DRUG use in PRISON

DRUG use in PRISON

Paul J Turnbull   Gerry V Stimson   Garry Stillwell

DRUG USE IN PRISON

Published by AVERT

11–13 Denne Parade, Horsham

West Sussex, RH12 1JD

Copyright © AVERT 1994

All rights reserved. No part of this publication may be reproduced, stored in a data retrieval system or transmitted, in any form or by any means, electronic, mechanical, photocopying, recording, or otherwise, without permission, in writing from the publisher.

First published 1994

British Library Cataloguing-in-Publication Data

A catalogue record for this book is available from the British Library

ISBN 1-898616-03-5

AVERT is a registered charity No. 296357

AVERT is a national AIDS education and medical research charity.

The aim of AVERT is to prevent people becoming infected with HIV, the virus that causes AIDS, to improve the quality of life for those already infected, and to work with others to develop a cure.

We rely on voluntary donations to support our AIDS education and medical research programmes. For further information about AVERT's work please write to:

AVERT, 11–13 Denne Parade, Horsham,
West Sussex, RH12 1JD

or telephone: (0403) 210202

Registered Charity No. 296357

THE CENTRE
FOR RESEARCH ON DRUGS
AND HEALTH BEHAVIOUR

The Centre for Research on Drugs and Health Behaviour is an academic research unit within the Department of Psychiatry at Charing Cross and Westminster Medical School. Established at the beginning of 1990, it aims to further the understanding of drug and alcohol use and related problems.

ACKNOWLEDGEMENTS

AVERT must be thanked for their continued support of our work on prisons. We are grateful, in particular, to Annabel Kanabus for her advice and practical assistance.

Milo Connolly, Jem Smith and Mark Lee are thanked for their assistance during fieldwork and analysis stages of the work. A special thank you to those who helped recruit respondents, especially Del.

We greatly appreciate the help given by the drug projects who hosted us while recruiting and interviewing respondents.

We would also like to thank the staff at The Centre for their practical assistance, support and advice throughout the life of this project. A special thanks to Daisy and Rosie.

Finally thanks to all those who gave their time to participate in the study.

CONTENTS

	Page
CHAPTER 1. Introduction and Background	1
CHAPTER 2. Drug Use	9
CHAPTER 3. Drug Supply	16
CHAPTER 4. Services for Drug Users	25
CHAPTER 5. Drug Injecting	33
CHAPTER 6. Drug Injectors and HIV	45
CHAPTER 7. Overview and Conclusions	53
References	60

CHAPTER 1

INTRODUCTION AND BACKGROUND

In 1991 we published the findings of the first study to report on HIV risk behaviour and HIV prevalence among ex-prisoners in England (Turnbull et al 1991). "Prisons, HIV and AIDS: Risks and experiences in custodial care" highlighted the unique nature of the prison environment for the possibility of HIV transmission, in particular the role of injecting drug use.

Drug use and injecting has continued within prisons, as have the associated HIV risk behaviours. Yet prevention practices and policies of the prison service in England and Wales have not kept pace. Prisons still remain a weak link in initiatives for the prevention of HIV transmission among injecting drug users.

AVERT and The Centre for Research on Drugs and Health Behaviour considered it important to continue research work on drug use and injecting in prison, first because of the scale of the problem and potential for HIV transmission, and second because of the current insufficiency of HIV prevention initiatives. Previous studies have described the significance of drug related issues within custodial settings. These have reported on the prevalence of risk behaviours such as the use and injection of drugs, the sharing of injecting equipment, and sexual behaviour. Epidemiological studies of risk behaviour informs the need for interventions, but must be supplemented by further examination and understanding of drug users and their drug using behaviour in custody. The research presented in this report aims to provide in-depth information that we hope may be of use for the development of HIV prevention initiatives, and the provision of education, help and treatment for drug users in prison.

The aims of this report

The data presented in this report are part of a broader study examining issues concerning drug use, HIV/AIDS and the criminal justice system. The overall programme is a series of linked investigative studies which aim to describe and assess responses in the criminal justice system to drug users and drug injectors in the light of HIV and AIDS.

The project described here examined drug injectors' behaviours and experiences within custodial settings.

The project had two main aims: first, to provide detailed qualitative information on drug use patterns and injecting practices within prisons; second, to identify opportunities for, and obstacles to, development of appropriate policies and practices to prevent the spread of HIV within prisons and to reduce other problems related to drug use.

This report deals with the five key areas which arose during the interviews, namely drug use, drug supply, services for drug users, drug injecting, and HIV infection.

Background

The realisation that large numbers of drug users and drug injectors spend periods of time in prison during their drug using careers has led to increasing attention to their behaviour and experiences while imprisoned. Official reports, research findings and press reports over recent years have highlighted high levels of drug use in prison and the risks and problems associated with the continued use of drugs (Report of HM Inspector of Prisons [1992]; Turnbull et al 1991; Covell et al 1993; Power et al 1992). Initial denial has been replaced by a willingness to acknowledge that these behaviours occur within custodial settings.

Drug users in prison

In England and Wales in 1992, 3,336 people were sentenced to some form of immediate custody for a drug offence (Home Office 1993). In May of the same year the population under sentence for drug offences was 3,158, or nine per cent of the sentenced prison population. Notifications by prison medical officers of inmates who were addicted were, at 2,586, 10 per cent of the total number of addicts notified from all sources.

Such figures only point indirectly to the number of drug users in prison, since many drug users are incarcerated for offences related to the financial demands of their drug use, rather than the possession or supply of drugs. On the other hand, not all those sentenced to custody for drug offences will be using drugs.

The most extensive study of the English prison population and drug using behaviour prior to imprisonment was conducted in 1988. This study found that 11 per cent of men and 23 per cent of women had been dependent on drugs in the six months prior to imprisonment. It was also found that seven per cent of the men and 15 per cent of the women had injected drugs in the six months preceding imprisonment (Maden et al 1990 a, b). It is estimated that overall, 7.5 per cent of the prison population in England and Wales at any one time (about 3,400 people) had injected prior to imprisonment, or 15,000 prisoners in any one year (Turnbull et al 1992, Advisory Council on the Misuse of Drugs 1993).

Many people who inject drugs have been in prison at some time. Studies have indicated that between 44 and 78 per cent of drug injectors have been in custody, and between 17 and 52 per cent have recent experiences of imprisonment (Keene et al 1993, Stimson et al 1988, Dolan et al 1990, Donoghoe et al 1992, Covell et al 1993) (see Table 1).

Table 1 Drug injectors reporting having been in custody

Location	Sample	Percentage in custody	
Wales 1990	165	44% at sometime	18% last 12 months
England 1989/90	829	57% at sometime	
E, W, S 1988	184	76% at sometime	39% year of interview
London/ Bristol 1989/90	207	55% at sometime	17% last 12 months
London 1990	533	71% at sometime	
Glasgow	81	69% at sometime	
Glasgow 1990	503	78% at sometime	52% last six months

Drug use and drug injecting in prison

A number of reports and studies have described drug use and drug injecting within prisons. While both are proscribed activities, it is clear that a wide variety of drugs are available in prison.

The use of some drugs, for example cannabis, is believed to be widespread. Her Majesty's Chief Inspector of Prisons, in his reports on the state of prisons over recent years has emphasised the extent of drug use in prisons. This report concluded that drug use in prison cannot be disassociated with the availability of drugs used in the wider community and that "society can no more expect total control over the presence of drugs in prison than elsewhere" (HM Chief Inspector of Prisons 1992).

In a study of the prison experiences of 452 recently released prisoners, 55 per cent reported that they had used at least one drug while incarcerated (Turnbull et al 1991). A variety of drugs were used; most common was cannabis but heroin use was reported by one in five.

Continued injecting and the sharing of used injecting equipment in prison has been documented by various studies conducted in England and Scotland (Dolan et al 1990, Donoghoe et al 1992, Stimson et al 1988, Turnbull et al 1991, Covell et al 1992, Power et al 1992). This wide range of evidence from England and Scotland suggests that between 23 and 33 per cent of people who inject drugs before imprisonment manage to inject at some time while they are incarcerated, albeit at a lower frequency than when in the community. In Scotland, in a random sample of all prisoners, eight per cent had injected at some time whilst in prison (Power 1992) (see Table 2).

Table 2 Drug injectors who report injecting when in prison

Location	Sample	Injected in custody
Edinburgh 1990	43	67%
London 1989	50	66%
Wales 1990	69	51%
England 1989/90	474	25%
E, W, S 1988	139	23%
London/ Bristol 1989/90	111	27%
England 1990	168	27%
Glasgow	56	25%
Scotland	154	25%
Glasgow 1990	262	16%

The limited availability of syringes in prison means that injecting equipment is normally shared (Stimson et al 1988, Dolan et al 1990, Turnbull et al 1991, Covell et al 1992). Studies have consistently shown that between two thirds and three quarters of all those who have injected while in prison share their injecting equipment (see Table 3).

Table 3 Drug injectors sharing syringes in prison

Location	Sample	Shared in custody
Edinburgh 1990	29	76%
London 1989	33	77%
Wales 1990	35	74%
England 1989/90	119	62%
E, W, S 1988	32	75%
London/ Bristol 1989/90	30	70%
England 1990	45	71%
Glasgow	14	43%
Scotland	43	74%
Glasgow 1990	41	73%

One needle may be passed between many groups of prisoners in different parts of a prison, often being exchanged for drugs (Pickering and Stimson 1993). The potential consequences of this continued risk behaviour for both the prison population and the outside community is of major concern (Farrell and Strang 1991, Brewer and Derrickson 1992).

Treatment for drug problems

In 1991 the Directorate of the Prison Medical Service, now the Health Care Services for Prisoners, produced a resource pack for people working with drug users in prison. The aim of prison service policy "is that the most should be made of the opportunity presented by imprisonment to help drug misusers break or modify their habit" (Caring for Drug Users, 1991). The "Caring for Drug Users" manual advocates a multidisciplinary approach and includes a recommendation for a short programme of methadone detoxification on reception as the normal response to a new detainee who has been identified as an opiate addict, unless contra-indicated.

It is currently difficult to gain an overall view of treatment practice in prisons, but it would appear that the availability of treatment for drug problems varies between institutions. Only some offer short detoxification programmes or counselling and advice, while others offer little or no treatment provision (Turnbull and Stimson 1993). An increase in the range of treatment options available within prisons and the creation of an atmosphere in which drug users will be more ready to ask for help has been suggested as key to dealing with problem drug use and the possibility of HIV transmission (Advisory Council on the Misuse of Drugs 1988, Turnbull et al 1991, Farrell and Strang 1991).

Prisons and HIV

Research on the prevalence of HIV infection in Western European countries suggests that injecting drug users are a critical link in potential transmission within prisons (Harding et al 1992). There is still, however, a remarkable lack of information about HIV infection within prisons, even though prison has long been recognised as an environment which is likely to contain disproportionate levels of those with HIV infection, and may also influence sexual and drug taking practices (Turnbull and Stimson 1993). While some anonymous screening studies have been carried out in prisons in London and Scotland, the prevalence of HIV infection among the prison population is unknown.

Previous AVERT funded research has described HIV prevalence and behavioural risks in prisons, highlighting the pivotal role of injecting drug use (Turnbull et al 1991). Using a sample of ex-prisoners, the study found the highest rates of HIV infection among those who had injected drugs before imprisonment: 15.5 per cent of women injectors and 7.7 per cent of male injectors were HIV positive. HIV infection was also identified in non-injecting women and in heterosexual non-injecting men.

In a study of a Scottish prison an HIV prevalence rate of 4.5 per cent was documented (Bird et al 1992), with a prevalence rate among injecting drug users of 25 per cent.

The consequences of injecting risk behaviour in prisons have been emphasised by the recent outbreak of HIV infection among drug injectors at Glenochil prison in Scotland. A screening exercise identified 13 inmates infected with HIV through sharing injecting equipment while imprisoned. This may be an underestimate of the real figure of HIV positive prisoners in Glenochil prison since not all prisoners undertook the test for HIV. It has been suggested that the number of HIV positive inmates in Glenochil prison could lie between 22 and 43 (Scottish Affairs Committee 1994).

The prison system in England and Wales has faced considerable criticism regarding its policies and practices on the care and treatment of HIV positive prisoners and the lack of measures to prevent the spread of HIV (Turnbull et al 1991, Farrell and Strang 1991, Advisory Council on the Misuse of Drugs 1988). Central to this criticism has been the policy of Viral Infectivity Restrictions (VIR) which allowed for the identification and segregation of HIV positive prisoners and those assumed to be HIV positive. The Directorate of Health Care Services for Prisoners has expressed the desire to phase out these restrictions and the number of prisons still operating these restrictions has diminished over recent years (Advisory Council on the Misuse of Drugs 1993). In a recent report, the Advisory Council on the Misuse of Drugs urged that VIR for seropositive prisoners should be formally abolished (Advisory Council on the Misuse of Drugs 1993).

Research strategy

Drug users who had recently been released from a custodial setting were recruited in a number of sites in three geographically distinct areas. By concentrating on recently released prisoners, it was hoped that problems of recall would be minimized and accurate information on recent conditions in prison would be obtained.

Interviewees were recruited through community based drug agencies, through existing contacts and drug using networks, and 'cold contacting' of drug users in drug dealing and using arenas (Power 1989). Interviews were carried out by one full-time researcher and two part-time assistants.

While the sample was not intended to be representative of drug injectors in contact with the criminal justice system, it was hoped that the use of multiple recruitment sites and strategies would provide accounts of a range of drug using experiences and varied contact with the criminal justice system.

The study was mainly qualitative in approach with some quantitative measures. Interviews with drug injectors were loosely structured and tape recorded, and aimed to elicit information about the:

- extent and nature of drug use in prison
- patterns of drug use
- social context of drug use
- environmental influences on drug use
- personal reasons for injecting
- situations in which drugs were injected
- strategies for protection from risk
- obstacles to safe injecting and discontinuation of drug use
- economic aspects of drug use and injecting drug use
- health effects of drug use
- treatment and help for drug problems – opportunities and obstacles.

Further research questions and issues were developed as the fieldwork progressed.

Analysis

Initial analysis of the tape recorded interviews was undertaken during the period when fieldwork was being carried out. The recordings were summarised and discussed among the interviewing team. The first interviews generated issues which were then taken forward to subsequent interviews. This was not possible on some occasions because of the opportunistic nature of sample recruitment. Further analysis, with the use of an index system, was carried out when the fieldwork had been completed. Some interviews (15) were also transcribed and analysed using the Ethnograph computer package for qualitative data.

Sample recruited

A total of 49 interviews were completed between April and November 1993. The majority (44) had been released between one day and six months prior to interview. Five interviews with people who had been released earlier than this are excluded, but will be used for other aspects of the research programme. The data presented in this report are based on the 44 interviewees who had recently been released from prison.

The majority of the interviews (28) were undertaken in central London. Eight interviews were undertaken in Surrey and a further eight respondents were interviewed in a Midlands town.

Half of those interviewed (22), including all of those interviewed in Surrey and the Midlands town, were contacted at a drug agency. Those recruited in central London were contacted primarily via 'networking' and 'snowballing'. Others were directly approached in street using and dealing arenas.

The majority of interviews were carried out in a key contact's or respondent's home. Other interviews were conducted in private rooms in a drug agency, at research offices, or at more public venues such as pubs, cafes and fast food restaurants.

The interview time varied greatly and was influenced by the differing accounts of prison experiences of those interviewed. The setting in which interviews took place also influenced the length of interviews: those undertaken in public venues tended to be shorter (between 30 and 45 minutes), whereas those conducted in interviewees' homes were longer (up to 165 minutes).

Profile of interviewees

Thirty eight men and six women were interviewed. Their ages ranged from 19 to 47 years, with a mean age of 28 years. The majority (28) described themselves as white British. Two described themselves as black British, three as Italian, six as Irish and two as Scottish. The majority were unemployed.

Most had been using drugs for a number of years. Age at first drug use ranged from 11 to 22, with a mean of 16 years. Age at first injection ranged from 12 to 36, with a mean of 20 years.

All of those interviewed used a wide range of substances prior to imprisonment. The majority primarily used opiates (39). The majority of those interviewed described and perceived their drug use as chaotic prior to imprisonment.

Of the respondents, 10 were receiving a prescription for methadone, four were receiving dexamphetamine, and one, a prescription for tranquillisers. Over half of those receiving a prescription also had contact with syringe exchange schemes and drugs information and advice services. For many (14) their only contact with treatment agencies was a needle exchange, 15 had no contact with treatment agencies prior to imprisonment.

The type of offence for which the majority of interviewees had been sentenced was theft, including handling stolen goods, fraud and forgery (16). Many were also imprisoned for drug offences (11). Others were imprisoned for offences relating to burglary (5), robbery (2), violence (3), or other offences (7).

Experience of imprisonment

The majority (40) had been in prison between two and fifteen times, with a mean of five times. For four of those interviewed it was their first experience of imprisonment. The mean length of last imprisonment was 22 weeks, with a range of two days to 18 months. The interviewees were held in different institutions throughout England; most had been in at least two different prisons. Interviewees were imprisoned in a total of 22 different prisons.

CHAPTER 2

DRUG USE

This chapter looks at the extent of drug use, and the reasons given for continuing drug use.

Throughout the interviews prisons were depicted as places where drugs were readily available but where the norms and practices associated with drug use were significantly different to those outside. As Tommy, a 30 year old who served an 18 month sentence, stated:

> "Yeah it wasn't like on the street. . . it was another subculture. . ."

THE AMOUNT AND RANGE OF DRUGS IN PRISON

The respondents' reports on the amount and range of drugs available in prison contained a common set of comments and observations, to the effect that prisons were places where drugs and drug use, rather than being uncommon or hidden, were difficult to avoid.

> ". . . what happened was the girl I was banged up with. . . she was getting parcels. . . like sixteenths and eighths [ounces of heroin]. . . and she was selling gear [heroin] in the prison. . ." (28 year old female, held in a London prison)

> "They sell drugs in every prison: heroin, hash [cannabis], everything." (29 year old male, imprisoned for 13 months)

> "I have never seen a prison so stuffed full of drugs. . . I said 'I'm after a draw, so can you get us a draw?', he goes 'I can get you anything you want from smack [heroin], coke [cocaine], rocks [crack cocaine], Es [ecstasy], acid [LSD], whatever.'" (29 year old male, held in a prison in northwest England)

Some interviewees believed that drugs were readily available at all times.

> "It took me 30 minutes before I got drugs on the inside." (24 year old male, imprisoned for three months)

> "Drugs were easy to get because parcels were coming into the prison and visits were easy to arrange." (33 year old male, held in a prison in northwest England)

Even if descriptions such as those noted above are treated as exaggerations, they still suggest that the quantity and range of drugs available in prisons is considerable. Such a perspective is supported by the more detailed accounts of the amount and variety of drugs that the respondents had personally brought into or obtained in prison.

"I was buying crack. . . on top of what I brought in. . ." *(33 year old male, held in a London prison)*

"I reckon I scored gear [heroin] about four or five times. . . when I was in there. . . and I scored hash about. . . probably about the same number of times. . . I got. . . pills and stuff. . . Valium, Temazepam. . . I got a couple of Rohypnols at one stage. . ." *(27 year old male, imprisoned for six months)*

All respondents had used drugs when they were last in prison. The most commonly used drug was cannabis, used by all respondents. The majority (36) used heroin and/or opiate substitutes over the same period, 28 had used a variety of tranquillisers or anti-depressants, six had used crack or cocaine, two reported using amphetamines and two had taken hallucinogens (see Figure 2.1).

Nearly all (42) had used at least two different drugs during their last term of imprisonment, with the majority opportunistically using a mixture of drugs throughout their stay. However, it was also the case that all the respondents who had been using non-prescribed drugs before going to prison reported using less while in prison.

The picture that emerges is one of a range of drugs regularly available, but where individual levels of drug use decrease and patterns of use alter. For example, cannabis use may compensate for decreased opiate use. Drug shortages or 'droughts' were mentioned but were never described as being extensive enough to significantly effect their overall level of drug use.

Figure 2.1 Drugs used by respondents in prison

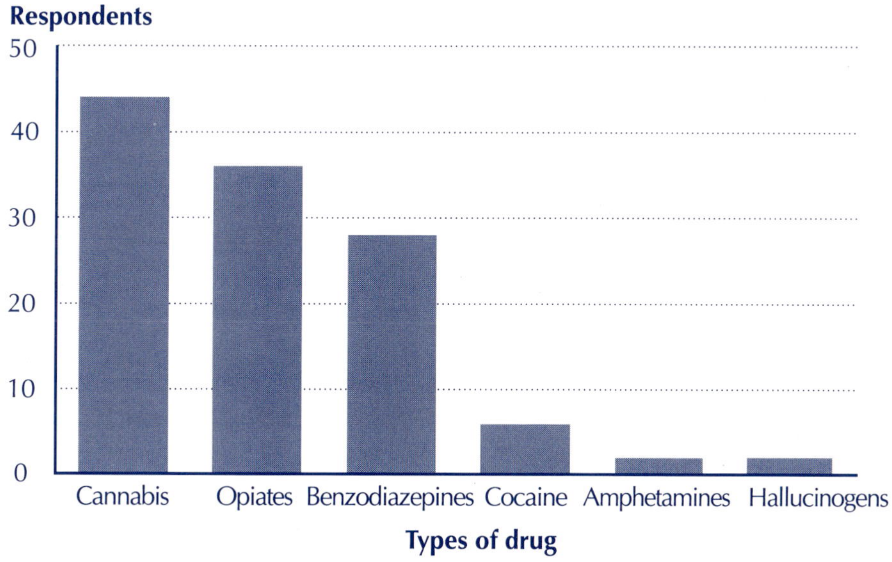

Drug preference

The majority of the respondents expressed a preference for cannabis, or for narcotics such as heroin, or tranquillisers such as benzodiazepines. Cannabis was cited as "the best prison drug" by a number of the respondents while most said that they were less willing to use stimulants such as amphetamines.

> "Amphetamines in prison I think are utterly insane... I can't think of a worst scenario than to be speeding or tripping." (27 year old male, held in a central London prison)

> "I was offered some speed (amphetamine sulphate) but I didn't want it. I've done it (taken it) once before in prison, what a nightmare, never again." (37 year old male, held in a prison in northwest England)

The lack of means with which to buy or otherwise obtain opiates or benzodiazepines on a regular basis led many to make do with cannabis.

> "I didn't have any income... money sent in and I wasn't getting visits... I was offered both coke and heroin but refused, could have used anything but stuck with a bit of hash... having gone through all those withdrawals I didn't want to start all over again." (29 year old male, imprisoned for five months)

Heroin use in prison

The majority of respondents had been using heroin or a substitute (methadone) prior to their last period of imprisonment. A small number (4) who had a good and regular source of supply and who were serving relatively short sentences managed to maintain their heroin use without interruption while in prison.

> "I used every day after the first day... I got a quarter on credit and then my girlfriend brought me two grams and 100 pills on a visit." (25 year old male, held in a central London prison)

> "I was only short for a couple of days out of the entire three months... it was only a couple of £5 joeys [bags of heroin] a day... it was about keeping straight... not getting out of it..." (31 year old male, held in a central London prison)

Most reported that they carried on using opiates after withdrawing when they first came into prison, but attempted to do so in such a way that they did not get a 'habit' (become physically dependent) again.

> "Yeah I was using (drugs) every day... but what happened was although I was using heroin... I was watching myself cause I knew I could easily get a habit... so I was being careful... taking downers [benzodiazepines] and smoking draw." (28 year old female, held in a central London prison)

> "... yeah but I wasn't using it regularly... more as a treat now and again." (34 year old male, imprisoned for six months)

However, nearly all (39 out of 44) of the respondents experienced withdrawal symptoms during their last period in prison. Most described how they initially invested a great deal of effort to ensure a supply of opiates but were not able to maintain a continuous supply.

> "He couldn't do nothing for me, he could get it [heroin] but I needed either money, burn [tobacco] or the lad said he'd swap it for temazies [temazepam], and I said... I had nothing, I haven't got a bean... so I'm stuck, pacing." (29 year old male, imprisoned for 12 months)

Some respondents experienced recurring bouts of withdrawal symptoms. Dave, a 28 year old man, who was imprisoned for 18 months, described how he was 'sick' (withdrawing from drugs) at different times throughout his imprisonment. He would find a source of money or heroin which would last for a limited period of time ending when the supply ran dry or he, or the prisoner supplying the heroin, was moved to another wing or prison. He would then experience withdrawal symptoms again until he found a new source of money or heroin.

The sites where drugs are used

Some drug use occurred in exposed sites, which were more public places within the prison, for example landings, exercise yards or visiting areas. Two explanations were offered for using drugs in relatively risky places. The first emphasised the social nature of drug use in prison.

> *"You know, you might be going round out on exercise after my visit. . . and I'll take a joint [cannabis cigarette] out on exercise with my mate who had been in there a while." (27 year old male, imprisoned for six months)*

The second – and more commonly offered explanation – was that it was a necessity due to the nature of the drug supply routes, as in the case of a man whose wife would bring in methadone:

> *". . . you know, you sit on your visit and a cup of tea and that, well my wife used to pour 40 ml of meth [methadone] in the tea you know. . . and I'd just drink it." (29 year old male, imprisoned for nine months)*

James, a 33 year old man held in a central London prison, recounted how his wife injected heroin into his thigh during a visit. They sat facing each other at a table. He crossed his legs so that the inside of his thigh was exposed and his wife inserted a needle into his thigh and injected the heroin.

Most drug use took place in the locked cells and dormitories where prisoners spend most of their time and the risks of discovery by the prison authorities are minimised. The most common and popular time reported was last thing at night after 'lock-up'. This was considered to be the time when the risk was lowest, and also enabled the use of drugs to aid sleep. It was also here that most of the injecting took place.

> *"We'd be careful. . . you know, getting ready to block the door. . . give us time to get rid of it. . . we'd take turns, he [interviewee's cell mate] would stand with his back to the spy hole when I was using then I would do it for him." (34 year old male, held in a prison in northwest England)*

> *"Yeah, always when you have more time, usually in jail they lock you in the morning, after breakfast, then we're locked in again, if we're washing up, so you'd wait until the last time they lock you up so you have more time to take your drugs, so in the evening." (27 year old male, held in a central London prison)*

Reasons for using drugs

During the course of the interviews all the respondents gave reasons for using drugs in prison. Some spoke of drug use as being a 'natural' and fundamental behaviour for them, and rejected the idea that they would stop using drugs just because they were in prison.

> "I am a drug user and therefore I will dabble, you know." (28 year old male, held in a central London prison)

> "I use drugs, doesn't matter where I am. . . if I can get them, I use." (33 year old male, held in a central London prison)

The respondents rarely spoke of their drug use in prison as being a positive and euphoric experience, except in relation to cannabis use.

> "I'd just do a bit of hash, just at night to get stoned, you know, and read a good book, you know, it was home from home, you know what I mean." (27 year old male, served four months)

> "Just hash. It is the best prison drug, was all round you, they let it go on to a certain extent but behind closed doors, if you've got a bit of hash you just mellow out and that." (29 year old male, imprisoned for 13 months)

John, a 32 year old man who was imprisoned for nine months in prisons in northwest England, believed that using cannabis was important to relieve the stress of being imprisoned.

Self-medication

Most of the reasons for using drugs in prison were couched in terms of the drug use being unavoidable. It was considered to be necessary as 'self-medication' to stave off or ameliorate withdrawal symptoms. These respondents thought their drug use was justified because when withdrawing from opiates, the insomnia and other symptoms they suffered made them feel as if they were "doing double time".

> "When I was first banged up I was clucking [withdrawing] so much I would have ripped someone's head off for a bit of gear [heroin]. . . you end up bargaining for other drugs. . . not for the buzz, just to sort you out [help with withdrawal effects]. . . while you're out there on exercise you are bargaining for anything you can get to help you sleep." (31 year old male, imprisoned for two years)

> "My wife come up and visit me, I said to her, I said listen, I need heroin in here, I cannot cope with this stuff [medication] they're giving me." (29 year old male, imprisoned for nine months)

> "The medication helped a bit. . . but I had my own little bit of gear. . . used that to take the edge off a bit. I only had little bits of gear though. . . so I kept getting sick." (27 year old male, held in a central London prison)

When speaking of a later, less acute stage of withdrawal, the respondents described how they still 'needed' something to help them sleep. The whole withdrawal process was reported by the respondents to last on average between two and four months, whereas they reported that medication for opiate withdrawal was provided for a maximum of 14 days.

> "I didn't get my head down for about three and a half months. . . before I got like a four or five hour proper sleep." (28 year old female, held in a central London prison)

> "I knew that my turkey [withdrawal] had gone like, just that my sleeping pattern wasn't back, I'd had a draw near enough every night." (29 year old male, imprisoned for 14 months)

> "I was taking downers. . . and smoking draw basically. . . and I done that. . . but by this time I was better. . . and I was gradually getting my sleep back. . . it still took about two or three months to get my normal sleep pattern back." (28 year old female, held in a central London prison)

Even those who did not refer to their drug use as a direct consequence of withdrawing from opiates or substitute drugs, still spoke of their drug use as necessary to help them get to sleep. The causes of insomnia most commonly cited in this context were anxiety, depression, boredom and physical inactivity.

> ". . . insomnia. . . boredom. . . general neurosis. . . I was really depressed. . . you know. . . after a while I needed something [drugs]." (27 year old male, imprisoned for six months)

> ". . . yeah that is what everybody does. . . just for the nights' sleep. . . because nobody's. . . you know if you are used to doing a day's work. . . and that. . . and just mooching about all day. . . you obviously can't sleep. . . so that. . . I think the main thing is insomnia. . . is one of the main driving things that makes people take drugs in prison. . . so that they can sleep." (33 year old male, held in a central London prison)

> "It [drug use] broke up the boredom and monotony. . . you're locked up for 23 hours. . ." (29 year old male, held in a central London prison)

Detoxification

Four respondents, two of whom were in prison for the first time, attempted to use prison as a place to stop using drugs, or at least have a rest from the type of drug use and lifestyle they had outside of prison.

> "Prisons are the best detox in the world – two weeks and you're off." (27 year old male, imprisoned for six months)

> "I felt like I had to use the time in prison as a rest from drugs, it's a good way you know, a lot of people I know who've been in prison, and they've come out before, have come out better for the rest, it's a good time to use it to recuperate." (33 year old male, held in a central London prison)

However, while these four respondents set out to use their time in prison in a constructive way, they all reported that their endeavours were far from successful. They stated that the quantity of drugs available in prison, combined with the lack of support and understanding on the part of the prison staff, made abstinence difficult. All them spoke about their drug use in prison as if they really had no alternative.

"I think deep down inside I wanted to get off them [drugs]... to come off them... but in that situation... and in that environment... I knew I couldn't do it on my own... even though deep down I wanted to come off." (27 year old male, held in a central London prison)

"There is a lot of hard drugs in prison and the temptation's... it's so easy to sort of carry on your use when you go into prison." (33 year old male, held in a central London prison)

"The whole thing is when you force somebody... a user to come off like that in there... there is absolutely fuck all point in doing that... the motivation has got to come from within..." (27 year old male, imprisoned for six months)

SUMMARY

Prisons are described by the respondents as places where a variety of drugs are re available and drug use is impossible to ignore.

All the respondents continued using drugs while in prison. Four people, two of whom were in prison for the first time, attempted to use prison as a place to stop using drugs but the quantity of drugs available, combined with the lack of support, made abstinence difficult. On an individual level the amount of drug use decreased and the types of drugs used altered in line with the reduced opportunities for obtaining drugs.

Respondents gave substantial reasons for their continued use of drugs while they were incarcerated. Some saw drug use as a 'natural' and fundamental behaviour for them and dismissed the idea that they would stop using drugs just because they were in prison. Most thought that using drugs in prison was unavoidable and necessary, particularly in the first few weeks or months, to alleviate withdrawal symptoms or longer term insomnia experienced as a result of their withdrawal from opiates or opiate substitutes.

Most of the respondents were opiate users and experienced withdrawal when in prison. There are generally inconsistent supplies of opiates in prisons. The respondents described two ways of coping with this: the first was to carry on using opiates as and when possible and risk withdrawal, the second and more common way, was to use cannabis more extensively and opiates intermittently. The main exception to this latter strategy was when the respondent was experiencing severe withdrawal symptoms.

Prisons constitute unique surroundings for drug use. There are diverse sites where drugs are used, each offering differing levels of risk of discovery, chances for association and opportunities to obtain and use drugs, which in turn influence the type of drugs used and routes of administration.

CHAPTER 3

DRUG SUPPLY

This chapter looks at the ways in which drugs enter into prison, and how prisoners obtain and maintain their supplies of drugs.

Drugs enter into prison in a number of ways. The main sources described by respondents were drugs being brought in by the prisoners themselves on entry into the prison, through personal visits, and within prisons from other prisoners who had access to drugs. Other, more opportunistic, methods of obtaining drugs were mentioned by several interviewees.

Entry into prison

Seven respondents concealed drugs upon themselves. Most concealed them intra-anally (in the anal passage), some swallowed them in packages, and some held them in their mouth. Intra-anal concealment was such a common practice that colloquially it was known as 'bottling'.

A 28 year old male from London who was on police bail before being sentenced to prison, made contingency plans on the day of his court appearance to continue his supply of drugs .

> "I thought I was going to get bail, I still bottled though. I had 150 Valium in a Durex, I pushed Physeptone up my anus, a couple of amps, couple of concentrates, and some bags of heroin." (31 year old male, remanded for three months)

Interviewees concealed drugs upon themselves in anticipation of a lack of supplies in prison, and because they thought any medication offered would be inadequate and not help the withdrawal effects they expected to endure.

Drugs which had been brought in by a new prisoner would sometimes be shared, and in return a future supply of drugs to the other party would also be shared. An alternative was the partial sale of drugs for goods or money that could be exchanged at a later date.

> "Yeah, as soon as you get in there, they'll come to ya to see what drugs you've got, to see if you're selling any." (29 year old male, held in a prison in northwest England)

Visits

Sentenced prisoners are allowed an outside visitor every two weeks while remanded prisoners can have a visit every weekday. The most frequently mentioned supply of drugs was through prison visits from friends and family. Twenty one interviewees reported receiving drugs during a visit on at least one occasion.

> *"My girlfriend or brother usually brought me drugs on visits. I either swallowed or 'bottled' the drugs."* (25 year old male, held in a central London prison)
>
> *"I brought in drugs into prison, I 'bottled' them, these lasted for four days. When these drugs ran out my girlfriend brought in drugs on visits every two weeks."* (24 year old male, held in a central London prison)
>
> *"At least twice a month I was brought heroin in on visits, from £25 bags to one gram bags."* (24 year old male, held in a central London prison)
>
> *"I got visits from my brother who brought me in gear. It took two weeks to get my own supply into prison. My brother usually brought me an eighth."* (27 year old male, imprisoned for six months)

An interviewee remanded to a prison in close proximity to the area in which he lived was able to maintain an almost daily supply.

> *"I was sweet, I was using throughout my time. I was getting my visits every day. . . apart from Saturday and Sunday, sweet as a nut."* (33 year old male, remanded for three months)

Strategies for maintaining a drug supply

Supply routes were often precarious with a number of aspects of the prison environment influencing drug supply. All interviewees relied on multiple supply routes at different points of imprisonment.

Once initial supplies of drugs which individuals brought with them on entry had been exhausted, the majority of interviewees maintained their supply through a constant interplay of internal prison sources and individual supplies through visits (see Figure 3.1).

Access to drugs depended on factors such as employment and freedom of movement within a prison. Many interviewees commented that they were able to gain access to drugs and the means to purchase them through their prison job.

> *". . . if you do not have a job, you are banged up for 23 hours a day and it is very difficult to get access to drugs."* (32 year old male, imprisoned for 10 months)

Drug supply through visits is vital to the drug market in prisons. Drugs are shared, borrowed and sold on the strength of a secure supply through visits. Respondents were able to use access to drugs through visits as a device to negotiate a more regular supply of drugs than their visits afforded them.

Figure 3.1 Obtaining and maintaining a drug supply

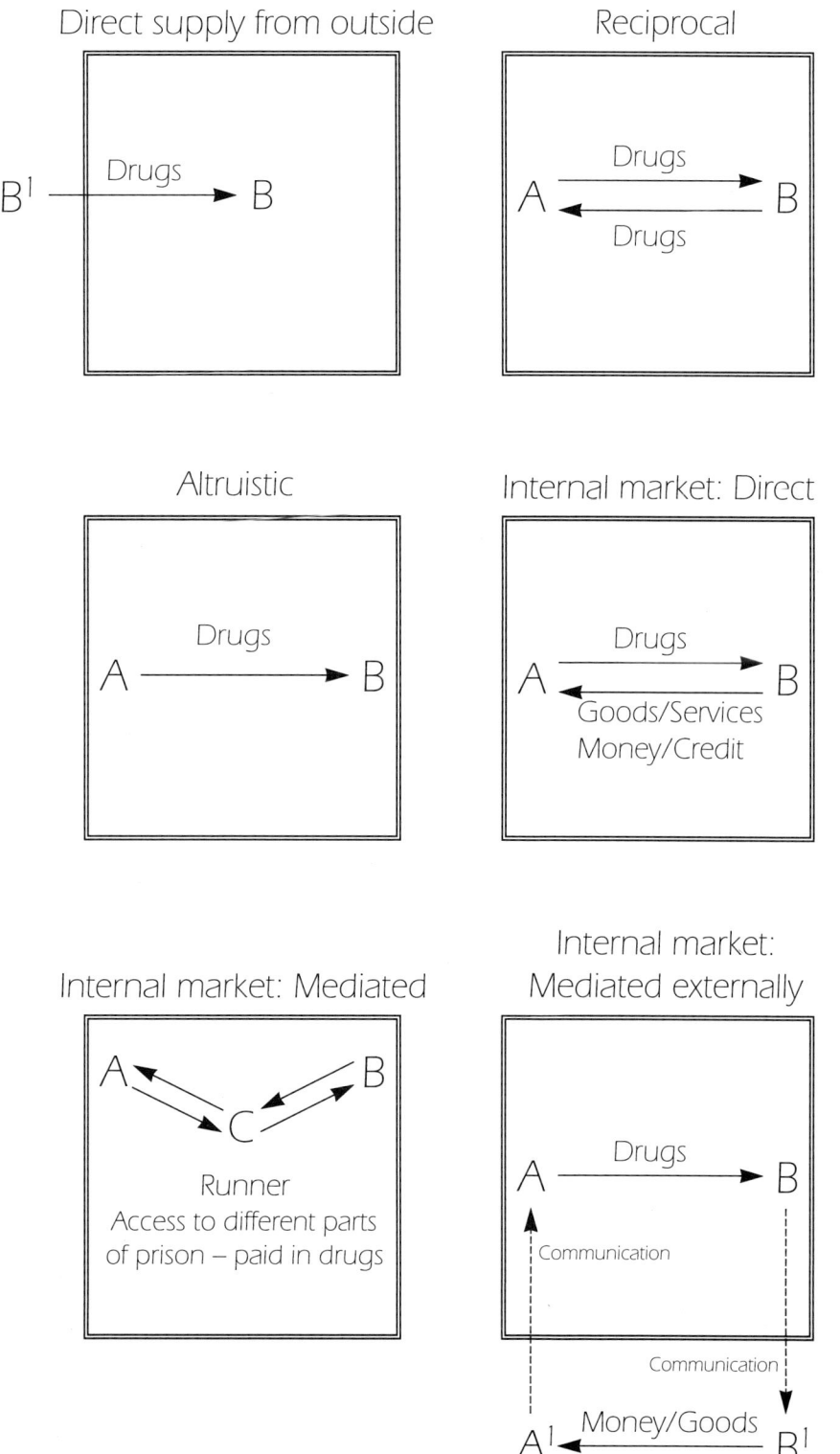

Locating a supply route within a prison

Many respondents were able to establish a supply of drugs within a short time. Friends and acquaintances from outside prison and from previous periods of imprisonment were often a source. Who you knew was important.

> "Two days later I get taken over to F wing, as soon as I get over there I'd see like, five people I know from in jail, so I've gone like 'listen I'm strung out, I'll have anything you can get me except draw.'" (27 year old male, held in a central London prison)

For those who had no such contacts other strategies were employed. For example, a 29 year old male interviewee could smell heroin being smoked on the landing on which he was held. He described trying to identify who was using heroin by simply looking for someone who looked like a drug user.

> "I got access to drugs in prison by looking for somebody who looked like a junkie. . . I got money through visits. . . it was an opportunistic supply." (27 year old male, imprisoned for six months)

An Italian interviewee described how it took him some time to establish a contact. He watched the activities of other prisoners and by this method identified the source of drugs. He approached the individual, offered him a cigarette and struck up a conversation. Two days later he purchased heroin from him.

Martin, a 29 year old man from Liverpool held in a prison in northwest England, on his first day in prison was collecting his evening meal when the man serving the food asked him if he was "after anything". Martin, being cautious, asked him what he meant and the man replied "drugs". Martin then asked if he could get him some cannabis. The man serving the food replied "I can get you anything you want from smack, coke, rocks, Es, acid, whatever." When Martin asked what the heroin was like, he answered "I can get you weighed bags, quarters, half grams, grams, quarter ozzies [ounces], half ozzies. . . all good stuff."

The cost of drugs

There did not appear to be any standard price for drugs. Costs varied greatly but most interviewees reported that prices inside prison were generally higher for smaller quantities of drugs than outside.

> "Drugs cost two times the amount they cost on the outside." (25 year old male, held in a central London prison)

> "£20 worth of heroin inside was worth £5 outside." (37 year old male, held in a prison in northwest England)

> "£5 bag on the outside is worth £8 inside." (22 year old male, held in a prison in northern England)

Paying for drugs

Money was rarely exchanged for drugs. Cash was used occasionally when respondents were held in open prisons, or when cash transactions could be facilitated on the outside.

One interviewee who was imprisoned outside the region in which he lived, away from his friends and family, found it difficult to get money to his drug supplier in prison. After a while he contacted friends outside prison who were then able to give money to the drug supplier's contacts on the outside. When the transactions outside prison had been completed the respondent received his supply of drugs.

Many alternatives to cash were used including telephone cards, confectionery, food, tobacco and other drugs.

> "Phonecards were exchanged for drugs, four phonecards for a bag of smack [heroin], two joints [cannabis cigarettes] cost a £4 phonecard." (28 year old male, held in a prison in northwest England)

> "I bought £10 worth of things from the canteen and I got a bag of heroin." (38 year old male, held in a central London prison)

> ". . . money's no good to people really, in jail, you know, the currency is either burn [tobacco] or drugs, that's what you barter with, either tobacco or drugs." (29 year old male, imprisoned for 13 months)

Many respondents supported their drug use by working, either through the financial rewards they gained from work or from 'errands'.

> "I was paying for the drugs out of the wages I received from my prison job. . . I got paid two £4 phonecards as wages. I bought smack once a week." (28 year old male, held in a Midlands prison)

Having a job presented interviewees with the opportunities to do favours or errands in return for drugs. Some mentioned that the type of work they were engaged in also enabled them to become drug dealers. Cleaners and those serving food had more freedom of movement in prison and had contact with many prisoners.

A 25 year old man, held in a prison in central London, worked in the prison canteen and was able to give other prisoners extra food, and do favours and errands. In return he was given drugs.

> "If you have a job in prison you can become a dealer for someone, as this will provide you with access to the other inmates in prison. You can get drugs in exchange for dealing." (27 year old man, held in a central London prison)

> ". . . had a job on the hot plate and was able to become a runner for a dealer." (31 year old male, imprisoned for six months)

> "I also bought drugs with favours, jobs and things that I did for other people." (27 year old male, imprisoned for six months)

Some drug users supplied and bought drugs as a method of supporting their drug use.

> "I bought and dealt inside for another dealer. I received one free bag for every three that I sold inside." (29 year old male, held in a Midlands prison)

Others borrowed drugs and cash from dealers but had to pay a premium.

> "If you borrow from a dealer in prison you have to give him one and a half times the amount." (37 year old male, held in a central London prison)

Drug sharing

Drug sharing appears to be a particularly important way of ensuring a supply of drugs in prison. Respondents recounted numerous instances of drug sharing as opposed to drugs passed on for financial profit or increased 'returns'.

A number of reasons were offered for this:

- inmates hoped to receive drugs in return
- it was a way of showing camaraderie with fellow drug users
- it was a way of being part of the drug supply mechanism within a prison.

It was also clear that there was an expectation that sharing would take place. Sharing was a prominent part of the social etiquette of drug use.

> "Well what I was doing was like what normal people would do that were in there. . . just used to. . . I'd be happiest when I got my drugs. . . I would share with whoever I was closest to in the prison. . ." (28 year old female, held in a central London prison)

The main reason for sharing drugs was that the user would be reciprocated later, when they received their visit or obtained the means to buy some drugs. Some respondents used this type of profitless drug supply as a strategy by which they safeguarded themselves against lean times in the future.

> ". . . cause if you don't. . . when you ain't got them and they get theirs. . . yeah I'll give her, she gets good visits. . . so I get it back. . . so I'd give people who could give me basically. . ." (28 year old female, imprisoned for eight months)

> ". . . people coming up and. . . saying give us a puff and I'll give it to you back on my visit. . . and if I'm with my mate and he's been in there a little while and he'll say. . . yeah he's sweet cops [gets drugs] on his visit. . . give him a puff. . . right I'd say. . . you know people who have been in a little while, they know who is who. . ." (27 year old male, imprisoned for six months)

The 'able to return' criterion was not always rigorously enforced. Some of the respondents described how they shared drugs without the possibility of return.

> "Well if they couldn't give it to me. . . well you know. . . if they was in my circle then I still would because I was that type of person. . ." (28 year old female, imprisoned for eight months)

Much of the respondents' experience of drug sharing was within partnerships or through informal networks. They described partnerships of between two and five members, and informally connected networks with multiple members.

> "People I was in a dorm with. . . wasn't into what I was into so I didn't have to share it. . . but I shared it with another friend of mine. . ." (28 year old female, imprisoned for eight months)

> "When I was on the hospital wing I did make some friends who got visits. . . they used to help us out. . . I had a few. . . a few chases [smokes of heroin] while I was in the hospital wing. . ." (28 year old female, held in a central London prison)

> "You call it. . . it's your camp [a group of prisoners who share drugs], you call it your camp, my camp was the four guys from Glasgow and the scouser guy, that was the camp and every week one cops [gets drugs], one gets a visit, we all kept each other going, whether it be hash, Valium, temazies, a bit of scag [heroin]." (29 year old male, held in a prison in northern England)

One situation where the sharing of drugs was common and the forming of a partnership was almost compulsory, was between drug users sharing a cell. In such situations the pressure to share drugs is increased since the two or more prisoners might have to spend up to 23 hours a day in each other's company. The respondents described how they shared drugs and trusted individuals who they had not met before. In the initial stages of these forced partnerships a 'sounding-out' (assessment of partner) process took place.

> ". . . you have to be careful. . . you know. . . we sounded each other out. . . he said about gear. . . he had some. . . he was getting visits. . ." (28 year old male, held in a central London prison)

> "Well what it is, as soon as you get in there, you know, shake of hands, and it's usually 'what're you in for?' and I went 'burgs' [burglary] and he went 'are you a user?' and I went 'yeah, I'm into gear and that', and he went 'yeah I'm into gear' and I went 'are your visits sorted?', he went 'yeah, I get my visit next week', and I went 'do you get gear in or do you just get pot or what?' and he goes 'I get gear in', I said 'well I've got half a gram on me', I said 'I'll sort you out if you want any', he went 'yeah', I said 'I've got temazies', and he went 'yeah, I want temazies, any chance of doing me some temazies?' so I sorted him temazies and a bit of gear. . . yeah. . . I sorted him, he's your pad [cell] mate, who's ever with ya, you sort out, I mean the thing is you've gotta remember, you've gotta live with that guy." (29 year old male, held in a prison in northwest England)

Drug sharing was especially common when one of the members of the partnership was leaving prison. Both drugs and injecting equipment were passed on between partnership or network members. It was expected that an individual who was leaving prison should leave behind injecting equipment, drugs, and anything else that might be valuable to those remaining in prison.

> "I gave it [a syringe] to. . . I gave it to my cell mate. . . perhaps he could trade it. . . you know, you give away little things like that. . . I knew I had a few quid coming. . . I gave him the tobacco I had. . ." (34 year old male, imprisoned for six months)

> "Yeah and I left my cell mate half my gear. Just in case, 'cos I wouldn't get back to the prison again so if I did get released, I didn't think I was gonna, I said don't do it 'till I get back, I said give me until eight o'clock tonight, if I'm not back by eight it's yours." (31 year old male, held in a central London prison)

Sanctions

Sanctions were applied to those who were unable to pay a debt arising from drug use or reciprocate within a drug sharing partnership.

Jane, a 29 year old imprisoned for eight months was granted home leave to visit her young son. Fellow inmates put pressure on her to bring back drugs on her return to prison.

> ". . . now at this time all the girls in my dorm were users and they said to me, you can't come back without anything. . . but I said I haven't got any money . . . and they said you can go out and graft for it. . . I said I am going home to see my little boy and my family and she goes you cannot go out and come back with nothing, you're in prison, you know the score. . . you know how to work. . . she goes 'you can get the money and you can bring the gear back cause if you don't, what can I say. . . you know what will happen'. . . so really I was being bullied. . . yeah and it frightened me. . . and it got to the point where I didn't want to go on this home leave but if I didn't go I would be in the same shit as if I did go. . ." (28 year old female, held in a central London prison)

On her way back to the prison Jane attempted to steal some goods from a chemist so she could sell them to buy drugs but was caught by a store detective. When the police arrived Jane pleaded with the manager of the store and the police not to charge her. Charges were not pressed and the incident was dealt with by the prison governor. Jane was not allowed any further temporary release, visits from family and friends were 'closed' (closely supervised), and she was to be held in prison for a further seven days on completion of her sentence.

Many respondents were aware of inmates who had requested to be moved from a general prison location to another part of the prison because of fear of violence. Dealing in prison lends itself to violence and bullying.

> "There was this one guy had to get himself sectioned. . . ended up in the base [isolation cell]. . . because he ran foul of this dealer. . . the guy would have fucking killed him. . . or given someone some gear to do it. . ." (34 year old male, imprisoned for six months)

> "There were a lot of people who were on 43s [segregation wing], it's unbelievable, they'd put themselves on 43 because they owed so much to the dealers." (33 year old male, remanded for three months)

> "I'd seen, like, people disappear as in they were on the wing one week, the next week they were on protection 'cos they owed that much money out, see they were letting people go up to like £300, £400 debts so they'd end up going on protection, rule 43, or getting slashed. . . somebody had offered me money to slash someone. . ." (29 year old male, imprisoned for 13 months)

Summary

Drugs enter prisons in a number of ways. Many imprisoned drug users bring drugs in with them. Many obtain supplies of drugs through visits and from the internal prison market. Gaining access to a supply is usually unproblematic. Access to drugs is related to freedom of movement within prisons, partnerships, and networks of friends. Most rely on multiple sources.

The cost of drugs varied greatly but most interviewees reported that prices were generally higher for smaller quantities. Cash, telephone cards, confectionery, food, tobacco and other drugs were used as currency for drugs. Many inmates supported their drug use by working in prison. Others were given drugs in return for favours and errands.

Individual supplies of drugs are shared with cell mates and other prisoners in a reciprocal relationship. This helps to maintain supply. Such behaviour shows the interdependence of drug users in prison and reveals the existence of a sub-culture operating within a sub-culture, with its own norms and values.

Prison drug use, despite being of a lower frequency than outside, brings its own dangers including the use of adulterated drugs, debt, and the possibility of violence and bullying.

CHAPTER 4

SERVICES FOR DRUG USERS

Specialist drug services in prison are provided by the prison service and community based specialist drug agencies. Most care for drug users in prison is undertaken by the Health Care Services for Prisoners. Some support is also offered by others based within prisons, for example probation officers and prison chaplains.

The effects of withdrawal from drugs, as already mentioned, are an important factor influencing the continuation of drug use. Interventions at this point may help alleviate symptoms and the necessity to use illicit drugs.

The initial period of entry into prison is crucial because imprisonment affects drug users' intake of prescribed and/or illicit drugs. Often the time between arrest by the police to detention in a prison, either remand or sentenced, is rapid, but a short period of time without medication or illicit drugs can lead to considerable physical effects for chronic drug users. The alleviation of this state then becomes a priority.

Drug users' contact with prison medical staff

Every prisoner is seen by the prison doctor on entry into an institution. If offered treatment for drug problems, contact with medical services would be continued for between two and 12 days. It appears that only in exceptional circumstances was contact or treatment offered over and above this initial period.

The interaction between medical staff and drug users tended to focus on medication, and from the prisoner's point of view concerned whether, and how much, doctors were willing to prescribe. The circumstances in which the consultation took place were often difficult, the drug users were often in a state of withdrawal and their overriding concern was the alleviation of these symptoms. The respondents felt physically ill, frustrated and angry, while staff appeared exasperated at having to deal with their requests.

Many experienced a blanket response to their requests for help, and said that little consideration was given to individual needs.

> "I seen the MO [Medical Officer] and the Senior Prison Doctor. I said 'I'm on methadone', I said 'I'm not a heroin user, I've been clean for three years', they said 'you're all the same.' " (29 year old male, held in a prison in northwest England)

> "The doctor wouldn't give me anything. . . he said that prescribing any drugs would just replace one addiction for another." (42 year old male, imprisoned for two months)

Others received moral judgements about drug use, and in response to a request for medication, were told that withdrawal from drugs was not life threatening.

> " 'OK I know you're sick, but you are not going to die', that's what he said."
> (35 year old male, held in a central London prison)
>
> "I asked for methadone and got two pills for two days. I was very sick but the doctor just said it was my own fault for taking drugs." (29 year old male, imprisoned for three months)

Some interviewees experienced prison doctors' frustrations with the circumstances in which they had to practise.

Gillian, a 30 year old long term methadone user imprisoned for a shop-lifting offence, described how she was lying in a semi-conscious state on the floor of the prison reception area. The doctor expressed his anger that this situation had arisen and told Gillian at a later stage that he had lodged a complaint with the police who had been in charge of her care up to that point. The doctor told Gillian he 'pushed' for her to be able to receive a maintenance prescription of methadone, since she was only remanded in custody, but was unable to offer it because of institutional regulations.

Several interviewees described prison doctors' frustrations with the actions of their colleagues. This primarily concerned the distribution and administration of medication.

Clive, a 25 year old man held in a prison in central London disclosed to the prison doctor that he was withdrawing from drugs. He said that the doctor asked the nurse to give Clive methadone, but the nurse told the doctor that there was no methadone available. The doctor, in an angry tone, said to the nurse that when he had prescribed methadone on previous occasions some patients had not received their medication, and also told the nurse that because methadone had not been dispensed he had had to give 'injections' days later to help alleviate patients' withdrawal symptoms. The doctor then repeated his instruction to the nurse that Clive be given methadone. The nurse then took Clive to the hospital wing of the prison and dispensed 50 mls of methadone.

The use of the strip cell

Martin, a 29 year old man from Liverpool imprisoned for committing a burglary, described his encounters with prison doctors over a two week period. On reception into prison he informed the doctor that he had a long term methadone prescription and had recently been using heroin as well.

> "He [the doctor] said 'I'll put you on Heminevrin for two days', I said 'that's not going to help me', and he goes 'it's either that or nothing', so two days, I had Heminevrin for two days. . . next day I see the doctor again and it's the same story, Heminevrin for two days like."

By this time he had severe withdrawal effects including vomiting, diarrhoea, stomach cramps, night sweats and aching muscles. Martin went to the doctor every day for the next five days pleading for medication to help him sleep.

> "On the sixth day I went down, I collapsed in there, two screws [prison officers] just pulled me up and said 'get your act together, stop putting it on', the sweat pissing off me, I'm balking [vomiting], I'm stinking, I put my case across to the doctor and he goes 'get out', and I said 'I haven't slept now

> since I've been here' and I said 'I need medical attention', I said 'I'm in bits' [severe state of withdrawal]. . . I kept saying it every time I went, 'I know you can't give me methadone but you can give me something to (help me) sleep'. He didn't want to know, as simple as that, just said 'go away' and I went 'no', I said 'you've gotta do something', and then the next minute three screws came in and forced me over to the hospital."

On the hospital wing Martin was seen by another doctor. The doctor asked him whether he was withdrawing from drugs, if he wanted to be on his own and if he needed something to help him sleep. Martin replied yes to all of these points and was told to wait outside.

> "It was like it came from nowhere, two screws just grabbed me, 'in the strip cell' they said and they threw me in there. They said 'take your clothes', I said 'what's going on here?'"

They asked him to take his clothes off once more, and when he refused two prison officers forcibly removed his clothing. Martin again asked why he was being held in a strip cell and the officer replied "you're a heroin addict and you're staying in here".

A few minutes later the doctor visited him in the strip cell.

> "I said 'doctor, you said you'd give me. . . I'm in here, and you said you'd give me something to help me sleep', and he threw me a blanket, he goes 'that's to help you sleep.'"

Martin was held in the strip cell for a further seven days during which time he received no medication. During this time the severity of his withdrawal symptoms increased. On a number of occasions he attempted to find out from the governors who checked his cell, the reason why he was held in a strip cell. However, he was not offered an explanation.

Medication

Nearly all of those interviewed (39 out of 44) experienced withdrawal symptoms when they were last in prison, indicating some degree of physical dependence. Medication to aid withdrawal was not routinely offered to identified drug users on entry into prison. In all, 40 respondents said that they had asked for some kind of medication. There are a number of factors that appear to influence the decisions made by prison medical staff including clinical judgement, institutional patterns and needs, and individual moral judgements.

The response to a request for medication was sometimes met with an outright refusal. The most common reason for this was that the institution did not offer such a service.

> "I asked the doctor for help [medication]. . . he said 'we don't do that here.'"
> (25 year old male, held in a central London prison)

Two Italian interviewees who requested medication to aid withdrawal were told that no such medication was prescribed in English prisons.

Interviewees described the different approaches to treatment that were offered in different institutions.

James, a 26 year old injecting drug user from Manchester, was remanded to a prison in northwest England, then once he was sentenced, was moved to another prison in that region. When remanded he told the doctor about his drug dependency and withdrawal symptoms, but said that the doctor refused him medication and told him his pain was 'self-inflicted'. After being sentenced and allocated to another prison, he again mentioned his drug using history and the fact that he was unable to sleep. On this occasion the doctor gave him a course of Valium.

The delay between arrest and imprisonment was also given as a reason by medical staff for the refusal of medication.

Steve, an HIV positive drug user from Cambridgeshire, received a custodial sentence but was held in a police station for four days because the prison he was allocated to was full. During this time he was withdrawing from methadone. When he arrived at a central London prison he said that he explained his drug problem and HIV status to the medical officer. Steve was informed by the medical officer that if he had come straight from court he would have received a reducing dose of methadone over three days, but because he was in the police station for four days he said "well you've gone through the worst of it now". Steve continued to experience severe withdrawal symptoms for a further two weeks.

A few prisons, it was believed, routinely offered the same course of medication to all prisoners reporting drug dependence. A female interviewee described how:

> "When you're sitting in reception. . . when you first come in you go in to see the doctor and you tell him what drugs and that you've taken. . . but you could say you were using 100 grams a day and this and that and the other, but all addicts get the same medication. I was on 125 mls of methadone (before prison). . . and he gave me 25 mls to be dropped by five mls a day."
> *(28 year old female, held in a central London prison)*

Types of medication

Of those who requested medication (40) just over half (22) received some. The treatment given was either opiate substitutes, minor tranquillisers or drugs to relieve the physical symptoms of withdrawal. Within each of these groups there was great variation in the period of time over which medication was given and the amount prescribed. Several interviewees did not know what they had been prescribed or were confused about the names of the drugs.

Opiate substitutes prescribed included Physeptone tablets, methadone linctus and dihydrocodeine. All were given in reducing doses over two to 14 days, the most common being a five day period. Some respondents also received other drugs, primarily minor tranquillisers.

> "Five days quick detox from 40 mls of methadone and diazepam at night. Also Lomotil for my stomach." *(22 year old male, remanded for three weeks)*

> "Four Physeptone pills over two days." *(29 year old male, held in a central London prison)*

> "I got medication for three days, 15 then 10 then five mls of Physeptone." *(27 year old male, held in a central London prison)*

For some, medication was withheld for a short period of time, until further checking had been undertaken, or it became apparent that the person was experiencing withdrawal.

> *"When they had checked I was on methadone, I got 60 mls of methadone, reduced by five mls per day." (19 year old male, held in a prison in northwest England)*

> *"After five days I was incontinent and vomiting all the time. I was taken in front of the governor who said that I was not cooperating and I had refused a detox which I had not been offered. I was given 50 mls of methadone, reduced by 10 mls per day." (27 year old male, imprisoned for nine months)*

The majority of those who were offered medication were given Valium. Apart from one individual who was treated with Valium for one month, all other interviewees reported receiving it for three days. It was generally given in single doses three times a day for three days.

Other drugs administered to interviewees included Heminevrin, a drug used for withdrawal from alcohol, and Melleril. Some mentioned receiving a combination of drugs, which they called 'Duckhams', believed to be a combination of Tryptizol and Melleril, to relieve stomach cramps and vomiting.

> *"The doctor only gave me something for my stomach because I was vomiting." (42 year old male, held in a central London prison)*

> *"They gave me 'Duckhams' for stomach cramps." (25 year old male, held in a central London prison)*

The majority of those who received medication were located in the prison hospital until the course of medication was completed.

> *"The doctor said he couldn't give me much, he asked the medical officer what he should give me. The doctor gave me three DF 118s (dihydrocodeine) a day for three days and I was kept in isolation." (28 year old male, imprisoned for one month)*

Dispensing difficulties

Problems often arose with the distribution of prescribed drugs. Sometimes changes in staff led to a failure to follow through treatment. This was often a source of conflict. The two quotations below highlight some of these difficulties.

> *"I was given one Valium three times a day for three days. The doctor said if I was still having problems to ask again in three days, which I did, but I saw a different doctor who would not give me any more, even though I wasn't able to sleep for a further six weeks." (31 year old male, imprisoned for six months)*

> *"I was given methadone linctus. This treatment stopped after two weeks. I was in the hospital wing and when their shifts changed they might forget to give me my medication. The treatment was too sporadic to be of use and I was very ill from withdrawals." (39 year old male, held in a prison in northeast England)*

Strategies to gain medication

The most common approach to obtain medication was disclosure of the kind and level of drug use, an emphasis being placed on prescribed medication which had been received prior to incarceration.

Some interviewees went to considerable lengths to convince the prison authorities of the treatment they had received prior to imprisonment. Many gave details of doctors and services with whom they were in contact, in the hope that the medical services in prison would consult with these outside agencies. Others requested to see their own doctors from the community.

William, a 39 year old man held in a central London prison, who had been receiving a methadone prescription for two years prior to his imprisonment, requested to see his own doctor from the community, and was turned down. When he saw the prison doctor William informed the doctor about the treatment he had been receiving. The doctor prescribed 45 mls of methadone, decreasing by five mls per day. When the course of treatment ended, William still experienced symptoms of withdrawal and again requested to see his own doctor, and was again refused.

William's parents, after visiting him in prison, contacted the psychiatrist who had been treating him for over two years. The psychiatrist contacted the prison saying he wished to see William, but his request was refused.

Reasons for non-disclosure of drug use

On entry into prison the disclosure of information about previous drug using may determine the help which is offered. Disclosure of drug use for many interviewees was out of their control, for example if the offence they were charged with, or the conviction they had received was drug related. Many had physical signs of drug use, such as obvious injection sites on their body, or sickness relating to their withdrawal from drugs. However, some interviewees tried to conceal their drug use. Some did this because they feared an admission of drug use would lead to repercussions later in their sentence. The fear of extra surveillance was a particular concern.

> "I said I didn't use because I would be watched." (32 year old male, imprisoned for eight months)

Some also feared drawing attention to their drug use because they had drugs concealed upon them, or they believed that they would be able to secure a supply of drugs in prison and therefore saw no purpose in disclosing their drug use.

Expectations of the kind of treatment and medication offered in prison also influenced decisions to conceal drug use. Previous experiences of imprisonment were a strong influence. Those who were experiencing imprisonment for the first time had perceptions of treatment based on the experiences of their peers.

> "I knew, because I've been in before, that they don't do anything for you." (29 year old male, imprisoned for six months)

Robert, a 27 year old male held in a central London prison, was on a drugs charge so it was difficult to hide his drug use. He attempted partial disclosure by informing the doctor that he was only a casual user. Robert's reasons for partial disclosure were three fold. He thought that treatment would be difficult to receive, that it would be inadequate, and that he would be located on a hospital wing (which was undesirable).

> *"I didn't want the treatment I heard goes with that... the hassle you have to go through getting the drugs that they give you... and they don't give you enough ... I didn't want to be with loads of people who were really clucking [withdrawing] and all that... cause that makes it worse... people whining and moaning about it."*

The perceived negative aspects of disclosure outweighed the negative aspects of withdrawal without medication.

Self-denial of treatment, primarily because of the undesirability of being located on a hospital wing, was mentioned by five interviewees.

A 35 year old Scottish male was questioned on reception into prison as to whether he used drugs. He told the doctor that he was drug free because he was under the impression that all the drug users were put together on a hospital wing, did not receive much medication, and that he would have access to drugs in the main part of the prison anyway and therefore not have to withdraw.

Summary

The prisoners in this study were mostly well-established drug users who, by their own admission, were dependent on opiates and/or chronic users of other combinations of drugs. About a quarter had been in receipt of prescriptions for methadone before they came into prison, many of them had some experience of services for drug users, and many had previous experience of imprisonment. They were for the most part very familiar with the kinds of help and services that might – or might not – be available in the community or in prison.

Contact with prison medical services was experienced almost entirely in the early stages of imprisonment. Interaction between drug users and doctors focused – from the prisoner's point of view – almost exclusively on medication and the alleviation of withdrawal symptoms. Drug users perceived that doctors' judgements of them, and their circumstances, were often moral rather than clinical, the symptoms of drug withdrawal being viewed as the result of a self-inflicted problem, and being non life-threatening. They also reported that doctors often said that they were constrained by prison resources or treatment policy. Because respondents were often physically ill, frustrated and angry, and doctors were exasperated by both the prisoners and aspects of their work, the interactions appeared to be particularly conflicting.

Medication, when offered, was primarily to aid short-term withdrawal from drugs. Drug users attempted to influence decisions about medication by negotiating with prison doctors. There was a great variation in both the length of time over which drugs were dispensed and the quantities prescribed. Drug users, on the whole, believed that the medication and treatment they received was inadequate, and that they experienced severe withdrawal symptoms as a result. There appeared to be little consistency in terms of treatment and medication within or between institutions.

A number of barriers to service utilisation were identified by drug users and some decided to hide their drug use. This was influenced by their previous experience or their perception of the nature of the treatment and medication offered. The amount and type of medication offered (or lack of it) and location on a hospital wing were strong disincentives for disclosure of drug use and requesting help.

CHAPTER 5

DRUG INJECTING

The published research indicates that about 25 per cent of drug injectors manage to inject at some time when they are in prison, but at a lesser frequency than when they are in the community. It also indicates that there are greater risks attached to injecting in prison, with higher levels of syringe sharing.

In this chapter we look in more detail at the circumstances in which injecting and equipment sharing occurs. All respondents were injecting drugs prior to their imprisonment, but not all continued to inject when they were in prison. Of the 44 incarcerated injecting drug users who were interviewed, 16 had injected the last time they were in prison.

The extent of injecting

There was extensive awareness that injecting occurred in prison, both amongst those who continued to inject as well as those who did not. Many knew about injecting from direct personal observations of needles and syringes.

> "I've seen some of the syringes in prison and they are in a bad way." (29 year old female, imprisoned for 14 months)

> "I was offered used spikes." (35 year old male, held in a prison in northwest England)

> "I saw about 15 to 20 needles on my wing while I was inside." (28 year old male, imprisoned for two months)

> ". . . these two were injecting in front of me." (29 year old male, imprisoned for nine months)

Others were more indirectly aware of injecting because they had no actual contact with needles and syringes or those using them, but had heard about them from other inmates.

> "There was a syringe around." (42 year old male, imprisoned for two months)

> "Everybody knew where there was a set [a needle and syringe]." (31 year old male, held in a central London prison)

> "There were a lot of people injecting. People get bored." (39 year old male, imprisoned for 28 days)

But some interviewees thought that injecting was sometimes considered to be more extensive than it actually was. As one summed it up:

> "It's not as rife as you hear." (29 year old male, imprisoned for five months)

Others indicated that a taboo existed regarding injecting drugs in prisons because of the high risks of infection with HIV.

> "There is an anti-injecting ethos at XXX prison because of HIV/AIDS." (32 year old male, held in a central England prison)

The source and cost of injecting equipment

Injecting equipment was obtained from a number of sources. Whenever possible, before entering prison, interviewees concealed adapted needles and syringes on their person. During visits by family and friends injecting equipment was passed to prisoners. In order to conceal needles and syringes this equipment was modified. These 'cut downs' or 'sawn offs' were adapted from one ml insulin syringes.

The main source of equipment inside the prison was from other inmates.

> "I bought the works off the guy who supplied the drugs. . ." (27 year old male, imprisoned for six months)

> "I borrowed it off my cell mate." (28 year old male, held in a prison in East Anglia)

> "I swapped drugs for access to works and lemon [juice]." (25 year old male, remanded in custody for three weeks)

> "People borrowed mine and I borrowed theirs." (27 year old male, imprisoned for nine months)

> "My works were supplied by diabetics. . ." (29 year old female, held in a central London prison)

Interviewees also mentioned obtaining equipment from the prison medical facilities.

> ". . . people stole them from the prison hospital or surgery." (38 year old male, held in a prison in northwest England)

> "I stole them from the hospital when I was left by myself." (25 year old male, imprisoned for two months)

> "I got 'sawn off' works which I was told came from the hospital wing." (33 year old male, held in a central London prison)

Since injecting equipment was very rarely used only once, needles and syringes were retained and stored for future use, often until further use was impossible.

The fear of random searches meant that interviewees sometimes concealed injecting equipment upon themselves. One interviewee described taping his syringe to his clothing. Others kept equipment concealed intra-anally. One interviewee mentioned keeping his injecting equipment on the outside of his cell window ledge. If storage posed a risk, syringes were passed on, often in exchange for goods or money.

Needles and syringes have various values placed on them and there appears to be no common method of payment or price. A diverse range of payments were reported within and between individual institutions.

> *"I bought them for £2. . . yeah. . . well I could have alternatively. . . given him £1, used them and then given them back to him. . ."* (27 year old male, held in a central London prison)

> *"It [needle and syringe] cost me £4 from a diabetic."* (29 year old male, imprisoned for 12 months)

Often drugs would be exchanged in return for the loan of needles and syringes.

> *"I borrowed the needle from a girl in exchange for some drugs."* (28 year old female, held in a central London prison)

> *"The diabetic would keep the needles for a couple of weeks. . . and others would loan the equipment in return for drugs."* (28 year old female, held in a central London prison)

Other goods such as confectionery and telephone cards were also exchanged for needles and syringes.

> *"I injected. . . with a syringe which I bought off an inmate with biscuits and chocolate."* (19 year old male, imprisoned for three months)

> *"I paid for the drugs and the works with eight phonecards."* (25 year old male, held in a central London prison)

Needles and syringes that appeared to be 'new', in that they came in a sealed wrapper, were bought and sold at a premium. However one interviewee reported that sometimes these were 'con' works: the works had been used but then returned to their original packet and resealed.

Reasons for ceasing to inject

Many (29) of those interviewed said that they did not inject drugs during their last period of imprisonment though they had done so during previous occasions when they had been imprisoned.

A range of factors influenced this change in behaviour. These can be broadly grouped into personal choice (including an assessment of the risks associated with injecting), practical (including the problems of acquiring drugs and needles and syringes), economic (the cost of drugs), stigmatisation (the attitudes of others), and decreased overall drug consumption (absence of a 'habit'). In most cases the discontinuation of injecting was influenced by a combination of factors.

The length of period of imprisonment, previous experience of imprisonment and whether the interviewee was convicted or on remand, did not appear to influence whether or not an individual injected, though such links might be found in a sample of a larger size.

Choice – personal decision

> "It's [injecting drugs] not really my scene in prison." (28 year old male, held in a prison in northwest England)

HIV – fear of infection with HIV

> "I could've got a needle but I didn't want to share because of HIV." (35 year old male, held in a prison in central England)

> "It's [injecting] like Russian Roulette." (28 year old male, held in a central London prison)

> ". . . couldn't trust anyone, in terms of HIV. . . people didn't give a shit." (28 year old female, imprisoned in a central London prison)

Access – unavailability of drugs

> "I was offered a needle, but at that time I couldn't get the drugs." (31 year old male, held in a prison in central London)

Access – unavailability of equipment

> "There aren't a great many needles available." (32 year old male, held in a prison in northwest England)

> "I was only offered dirty needles, couldn't get clean ones." (35 year old male, imprisoned for 12 months)

Access – unavailability of good quality, clean equipment

> "I don't inject in prison unless I have my own syringe. Some of the syringes in prison are in a bad way." (29 year old female, imprisoned for 18 months)

> "Even if it looks new you cannot trust it." (28 year old male, held in a central London prison)

Economics – resources to purchase

> "I couldn't get enough money together." (27 year old male, held in a central London prison)

Stigmatisation

> "People who inject in prison can be stigmatised as HIV carriers." (32 year old male, imprisoned for nine months)

Decreased drug consumption – no need to inject

> "I never inject in prison, I don't have a habit by then." (32 year old male, held in a central London prison)

Reasons for continuing to inject

Those who continued to inject drugs in prison consisted of two main groups. There were those who indicated that they always intended to continue to inject, and there were those who continued or resumed injecting due to circumstances and immediate influences.

A personal preference for injecting was mentioned by a number of respondents. For these respondents, injecting was an important part of taking drugs.

> *"I'm an injector therefore if I'm going to use a drug I will inject it." (33 year old male, remanded for three months)*

But many other respondents had initially resolved not to inject drugs, but when needles and syringes became accessible they injected. The availability of drugs and injecting equipment appeared to be a dominant influence for continued injecting drug use.

> *"There were so many drugs around and new works. . . I just couldn't resist." (29 year old male, held in a central London prison)*

Mark, a 27 year old held in a central London prison for eight months, had arranged with the cleaner on his landing to purchase a £10 bag of heroin. He had done this on several occasions before and had always smoked the drugs. On this occasion when the cleaner brought the drugs he also brought a needle and syringe which he offered to Robert. Robert rented the needle and syringe for £2 on this occasion and continued to do so throughout the rest of his time in prison.

Frequency of injecting

The number of injections varied greatly. The frequency of injecting ranged from single isolated occasions through to regular twice daily injecting over a four week period (see figure 5.1). Patterns of injecting appear to be diverse. Four of those interviewed were unable to quantify how often they had injected.

The frequency of injecting appeared to be influenced by the availability, primarily of drugs, but also of needles and syringes.

Jane, a 28 year old imprisoned for eight months in a central London prison, described how her source of needles was a fellow drug user who was diabetic. During visits to the hospital wing for insulin treatment the diabetic, on the odd occasion, could steal and conceal syringes, and return to the wing with them. The insulin syringe would be available to Jane for three to four days and then it would be traded for drugs by the diabetic. If there were no syringes Jane would smoke her drugs.

Ted, a 28 year old imprisoned for six months in a central London prison, bought and borrowed injecting equipment from a fellow prisoner who was selling drugs. Ted was only able to have money brought to him once a month when he had a visitor, and could not get credit within prison. He bought heroin on five occasions and each time he injected it.

For those who did not have their own source of injecting equipment and relied on the prison market, the cost of equipment sometimes precluded injecting.

James, a 25 year old imprisoned for eight months in a central London prison, had been injecting regularly with a needle and syringe brought into prison by a friend during a visit. During a cell search the syringe was discovered by prison officers and confiscated. James, unable to secure another source of needles and syringes, tried to buy an unused set. He was told a new set in sealed wrapping would cost £10, a price he could not afford. With only two months of his sentence to serve, James decided to smoke his drugs for the remainder of his time in prison.

Figure 5.1 Patterns of injecting

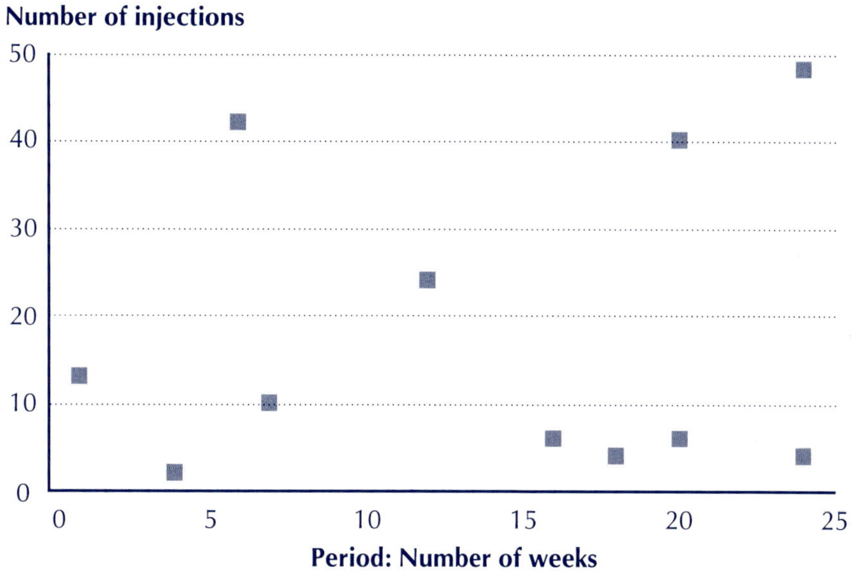

Number of injections vs **Period: Number of weeks**

Context of injecting

The context (the time, location and environment) in which injecting occurred was diverse. Again, most importantly, injecting was related to the supply of drugs and injecting equipment. These two factors appeared to have a considerable influence on when, where and how drugs were injected.

Many of those injecting in prison did so at irregular intervals, influenced by the supply of drugs, needles and syringes. When these component parts had been gathered together the actual injecting event was further influenced by a number of other factors. When needles and syringes were on loan, respondents had a limited amount of time in which to prepare and inject their drugs.

> "Washing up time, probably about 10 minutes. Before you were locked in your cell you had to wash it [needle and syringe], get an injection and give it back before they lock you up." (27 year old male, imprisoned for six months)

The most common time to inject was in the evening before the cells were secured.

> "Usually when you have more time, you wait until the last time they lock you up so you have more time for a hit [injection], so in the evening." (27 year old male held in a central London prison)

> "At night. . . everybody saves their drugs till then. . . you don't get the opportunity otherwise. . . just before they turn the lights off you get an opportunity to have a hit. . ." (27 year old male, held in a central London prison)

Often, however, drug injection was not pre-planned but opportunistic.

> *"As long as you can get the gear you inject as soon as you have a chance."*
> *(27 year old male, imprisoned for four months)*

The majority injected in the relative privacy of their own cells, and they often shared drugs in their cells. Some respondents injected in other parts of the prison in which they were held. Three mentioned injecting in the cell in which drugs and injecting equipment was purchased.

Dino, an Italian who was held in a central London prison for seven months, said that he injected when housed on a hospital wing awaiting the result of an HIV test. He was offered drugs and injecting equipment by fellow inmates in the hospital wing. They prepared the drugs together and took turns to take their share of the drugs and to inject. During the time he was on the hospital wing he injected drugs in the presence of 15 other inmates who were also injecting.

Injecting in the presence of others was sometimes perceived as 'unsafe'. It was seen as problematic when a cell mate's attitude towards drug users was not known or was known to be negative.

> *". . . yeah like I say, cooking up was a problem. . . once with this one guy I was with. . . because he obviously would disapprove. . . and I was worried about him starting while I was trying to do a hit. . ."* (27 year old male, imprisoned for six months)

This led to some interviewees trying to conceal their injecting practices from other prisoners.

Robert, a 27 year old male who was imprisoned in a central London prison for six months, recounted how he often had to inject drugs in his bed under a blanket.

> *". . . you can do it without them [cell mates] knowing. . . you know, lying down in your bed like that [interviewee imitates injecting under a blanket]."*

Robert went on to describe how the process of preparing drugs for injection was impossible to conceal, and this therefore made injecting hazardous since a disapproving cell mate could intentionally push over the drugs while they were being prepared.

The sharing of needles and syringes

Needles and syringes were often shared by prisoners. Of the 16 respondents who injected when last in prison, nine reported sharing injecting equipment at some time. There were a number of factors which influenced syringe sharing, and these were generally related to the immediate lack of availability of sterile injecting equipment and the need to take drugs. Sharing, including passing on, or the re-use of already used injecting equipment, was common and not an isolated occurrence.

However, the respondents had a very precise understanding of what 'sharing' meant. 'Sharing' was perceived to be time limited and related to the proximity of other sharers.

'Sharing' occurred if needles and syringes were used immediately after, or prior to, their use by another person. 'Sharing' was also seen as being dependent on the presence, when injecting took place, of others who were using the same needles and syringes. The term 'sharing' was rarely used to describe the re-use of injecting equipment that had already been used or the passing on of injecting equipment. If a period of time elapsed between the episodes of use, or other sharers were not present during injection, it was described as "just using old works".

The extent of sharing injecting equipment ranged from irregular occurrences to each time that drugs were injected.

Some only shared on a few occasions.

> "I got needles from somebody else a couple of times." (42 year old male, held in a prison in northwest England)

> "I injected twice with works I borrowed from a cell mate." (28 year old female, imprisoned for eight months)

A 27 year old Irish man, held in a prison in northwest England, injected regularly with equipment which he had brought into the prison himself. However while acting as an intermediary for someone supplying drugs, he used equipment that had been used by someone else on three separate occasions. He used other peoples' needles and syringes on these occasions because he wished to take the drugs immediately because he was experiencing withdrawal symptoms.

For others sharing was a more common practice.

> "I injected every second day, once a day with works I had to hire, which had been used by others." (27 year old male, imprisoned for three months)

> "Every time I injected – there aren't any new works in prison." (29 year old male, held in a central London prison)

A 37 year old man first injected when located in a hospital wing in a prison in northwest England. He shared on two occasions with three others also in the hospital during a two week period. When he left the hospital wing and was re-located to the main part of the prison, he continued to inject, and shared on every occasion, approximately twice a week for five months.

The frequency of sharing for some respondents was linked to the supply of drugs.

> "When I scored smack [heroin] I rented or bought works that had been used God knows how many times." (27 year old male, imprisoned for six months)

The frequency of sharing was influenced primarily by individuals' access to injecting equipment, which in turn was influenced by the resources available to an individual to purchase new needles and syringes, or the opportunity to secure a source of equipment from outside. The majority of those who shared injecting equipment rented or borrowed needles and syringes.

Injecting with equipment that had already been used was a last resort for a number of interviewees. When a supply of 'clean' (new) needles had been organised some injectors would only use their own works. Problems arose for those who had brought in needles and syringes, when the equipment became too worn out for further use. An interviewee who brought a needle and syringe into prison began to share when his needle became so blunt that it was damaging his veins. Another interviewee described how the needle he was using was like a 'rusty nail' and could not be used any more. He then had to borrow needles and syringes that had been used by others.

Jane, a 28 year old female injector was still having great difficulty sleeping, two months into her prison sentence. She was sharing a dormitory with a number of other women, two of whom were regularly injecting heroin. Jane explained to them that she was unable to sleep and expected to get drugs on the next visit from a friend, and they agreed to share what they had if she would do the same in return. The drugs were prepared in a spoon, drawn up through a makeshift filter, each taking a turn to draw up their share, quickly rinse the needle and syringe with cold water and then pass it on. Jane went last, and injected the small amount of drugs that were left, then boiled the makeshift filter to obtain the excess drugs from it.

Robert, a 27 year old student from London, rented a needle and syringe for £2 from a fellow prisoner who was also selling drugs. Robert gave the money to a landing cleaner who returned sometime later with the needle and syringe. It was obvious to Robert that the equipment had already been used since the needle was very blunt. He rinsed the needle and syringe before injecting. The needle and syringe were then returned via the landing cleaner to the drug dealer.

Sharing other injecting paraphernalia

Sharing has three component parts which risk HIV infection (Grund 1993). These are the sharing of needles and syringes; the sharing of other injecting equipment, such as filters, spoons or 'cookers'; and the sharing of drug solutions using methods such as backloading, by transferring some of the contents of one syringe to another (Jose et al 1993).

The sharing of injecting paraphernalia in prison is not restricted to needles and syringes, but includes sharing spoons and other devices for preparing drugs, such as filters through which drugs are drawn, and containers for water to flush out injecting equipment.

Tim, a 34 year old Irish man who was in prison for 12 months often shared injecting paraphernalia with his cell mate. Drugs and paraphernalia were shared but not needles and syringes. He and his cell mate collaborated in the preparation of drugs since they believed it was easier and safer than undertaking it individually. The drugs were prepared in a bottle top with "Jif" lemon acquired from the prison kitchen, and water from the tea urn. Tim described how his cell mate and himself would measure out equal quantities of the drugs they each had.

"I'd show him what I'm putting in and he'd show me. . . and I'd agree. . ."

The drugs were 'boiled up' together.

> "It's best for just one boil up. . . than two because it was taking twice as long and was leading to arguments. . . and the screws [prison officers] could walk in the door at any time."

The prepared drugs were then drawn up through a makeshift filter made from toilet paper into one syringe and a half share was then injected into another syringe (a process known as backloading). The remainder of the water was then used by both Tim and his cell mate to flush out their needles and syringes.

It was common for those with access to drugs to give the residue of drugs left from their preparation – such as the excess in the 'cooker', filter and syringe – to fellow inmates who did not have any drugs.

Cleaning injecting equipment

All of those who shared were aware of the risk of HIV transmission. When describing how they shared needles and syringes and other paraphernalia, they would also often describe the attempts they made to reduce the risk of HIV transmission.

Some attempt at cleaning injecting equipment was reported by all of those who injected. Attempts to wash out equipment were made by those who shared needles and syringes but also by those who injected with their own equipment. Some respondents mentioned that they knew and understood how to clean injecting equipment appropriately, but in prison they were unable to carry out this process effectively and had to adapt their cleaning practices.

> "When you got a cup of tea you could just as easily get a cup of water. . . one of us would get a cup of water. . . and the water was used and you would just flush it out." (34 year old male, imprisoned for five months)

> ". . . I'd do that by heating a little piece of soap. . . cooking a piece of soap down in a spoon so I had a mixture of boiling water and soap. . . flushed it through but I couldn't immerse the whole thing. . . that's the problem really . . ." (27 year old male, held in a central London prison)

The above interviewee went on to describe that access to water was sometimes difficult. On a number of occasions he used his urine from the slop bucket in his cell to supplement the water with which he cleaned his syringe.

Some mentioned that they cleaned their injecting equipment with bleach or other disinfectants.

> "Well you clean your cell out with bleach, you get some bleach in a bucket." (29 year old male, imprisoned for three months)

Another said how he had a bottle of "Dettol" because he had a scalp disorder, and he used this to clean his needle and syringe.

However, the quality of the cleaning methods was recognised by many as being inadequate for the prevention of HIV infection.

> "I would go to the sink and just go psss [sound imitating pushing water through injecting equipment] with water. . . just like that." (28 year old female, held in a central London prison)

The kind of needles and syringes most often used within prisons also precluded efficient cleaning, the most common type being one ml insulin syringes. These are designed to be used only once and have fixed needles.

> "You know the bottom of one mls, they're always one mls yeah, the blood at the bottom it always congeals at the bottom of one mls, doesn't matter how many times you clean it out, that bit of blood's there you know." (28 year old male, held in a central London prison)

The disposal of injecting equipment

Most needles and syringes appeared to have long lives. Many interviewees were unaware of how injecting equipment was disposed of, because this was such a rare occurrence.

> "I don't know how, if it was disposed of properly or if it was left in the cistern of the toilet or threw it out of the window." (29 year old female, imprisoned for nine months)

When one interviewee left prison he gave the needle and syringe he had been injecting with for several months, to his cell mate.

> "I just said maybe he could get a bit of gear with it. . ." (34 year old male, held in prison in northwest England)

> "I really don't know what happened to them, whatever their state I just sold them on." (27 year old male, imprisoned for six months)

Only one interviewee was able to describe what happened to old injecting equipment. He had a constant supply of needles and syringes throughout his period of imprisonment, and went to great lengths to destroy his injecting equipment so it was unrecognisable.

> "I used to melt the plastic and bang down the wire as much as I could or else I'd melt the wire if I had enough matches. . . it just looked like a burnt piece of black rubbish." (33 year old male, remanded for three months)

SUMMARY

A third of the drug injectors who took part in the study continued to inject when last in prison, including the 'intentional' injectors who had planned to continue injecting, and those whose injecting was more 'opportunistic'. Their frequency of injecting was less than prior to their imprisonment. However, injecting drugs was by no means an isolated event. The frequency of injecting was influenced primarily by the availability of drugs and needles and syringes.

Drug injection was often carried out within the confines of a prison cell in the presence of other cell mates. Cell mates were also involved in drug use and drug injecting. Needles and syringes were often borrowed or rented.

Of those who injected in prison over half (9) shared needles and syringes. The use of injecting equipment that had previously been used by others was common for many of this group. People who shared were likely to be those who did not have their own source of needles and syringes. Individual sources of needles were prone to 'droughts' which often led to sharing. The risk of HIV transmission through sharing needles and syringes was understood by many of this group, but they often perceived their behaviour as 're-use' and not as sharing.

The sharing of other injecting paraphernalia was common among all of those who injected in prison. Some drug using practices included backloading, sharing filters and water, and using residues from the paraphernalia, also carry a risk of HIV transmission within the population who inject in prison.

All of those who injected made some attempt to clean their needles and syringes. Injectors often perceived the process used to clean injecting equipment as being inadequate. Appropriate cleaning materials were not available. The type of needles and syringes likely to be used in prison also made efficient cleaning problematic. The conditions (length of time available and location) under which the cleaning was undertaken made the possibility of a comprehensive and thorough cleaning unlikely.

The disposal of previously used injecting equipment was rare. All needles and syringes were re-used. Interviewees retained needles and syringes for further use until they could no longer be used.

DRUG INJECTORS AND HIV

HIV infection is a difficult and sensitive area for prison staff and for prisoners. The Prison Medical Service and its successor, Health Care Services for Prisoners has, over the years since 1987, introduced a number of measures to try to improve the practices in prisons, and to educate prison staff and prisoners. These include a staff training package, a prisoners' training package, the training of prison staff from a range of disciplines as counsellors, and the development of a multidisciplinary course to encourage coherent practice at the level of the individual institution.

This chapter looks at drug injectors' recent experiences of issues related to HIV infection within prison.

EDUCATION AND INFORMATION

The Health Care Services for Prisoners has produced an education package on HIV which consists of a video which is then followed by a question and answer session. Prisons were advised that every prisoner spending longer than four weeks in prison should be given a chance to see the video. In addition, a leaflet about HIV and risk behaviour, designed by the Terrence Higgins Trust and the Prison Service, was to be distributed to all those in prison and all new receptions into prison.

The video

The majority of those who were interviewed reported that they had not received any information or educational activity concerning HIV and AIDS. Only nine of the interviewees said that they were shown the video and 31 said that they did not see it. Of those who had not seen the video, two had been offered an opportunity to view it but chose not to, because prison officers were present or they were suspicious about the attitudes of officers.

> "The video was once a week where you watched people injecting and ex-addicts with their faces covered saying 'don't use in prison because you're liable to catch HIV' or whatever, you know, but who's going to watch that with six screws there?" (29 year old male, held in a central London prison)

> "There was no information about HIV/AIDS except an AIDS film which was not made obligatory as the prison officers were too apathetic to make everyone watch. A lot of people wouldn't ask (to see the video) because of the way the screws [prison officers] would react. . . in a negative way." (34 year old male, held in a prison in northwest England)

Those who saw the video were shown it during the early stages of imprisonment, which accords with Prison Department aims that it should be shown within the first four weeks of imprisonment. There were some critical comments about different aspects of the presentation, and a number of interviewees felt that the video itself was of poor quality and that the information was not up-to-date.

> "They showed me the video on HIV during a three day induction course. The video is useless as it is out of date." (29 year old male, imprisoned for five months)

Others described problems with aspects of the presentation.

> "There was a film shown, but there was no discussion." (32 year old male, held in a prison in central England)

> "There was a video but there was no sound because the prisoners and the screws [prison officers] had seen it so many times that they were fed up with it. It was crap." (38 year old male, imprisoned for three months)

> "I saw the video about HIV – it was difficult to get anything from it – nobody was paying attention." (31 year old male, imprisoned for six months)

The leaflet

Only four interviewees were given the Terrence Higgins Trust leaflet describing HIV risk behaviour. However, two others reported that they had seen a leaflet in other prisoners' cells.

> "On reception I was given this leaflet. . . I read it, it's something to read. All things like that, it's a load of bollocks, it's just rules." (22 year old male, imprisoned for eight months)

> "There were some posters, I saw a leaflet about cleaning in somebody's cell. I don't know where it came from. I knew about all the stuff it had on it anyway." (27 year old male, held in a central London prison)

One interviewee was critical of the leaflet he received, believing the information on it could lead to disciplinary action for possession of injecting equipment.

> "There was a leaflet in XXX prison which advised you to keep your works in your tobacco box; you would be stupid if you did that, you'd get nicked." (42 year old male, imprisoned for five months)

Other sources of information

Several interviewees said that they had been given other opportunities to gain information and education about HIV, including discussions they had with probation staff, medical staff, chaplains and staff of outside agencies. Five interviewees described posters they had seen within the prisons in which they were incarcerated.

> "In this prison there is quite a bit of education, posters, leaflets. The officers are quite supportive." (29 year old female, held in a central London prison)

> "I went to an HIV awareness group – there were officers in the group too. There was one officer in the group who was homosexual; he got so much abuse." (29 year old male, held in a central London prison)

One 26 year old man, on entry into a central London prison, was given information about HIV by the doctor. The doctor also asked him about his sexual and drug taking behaviour with reference to HIV, and whether he wanted a test for HIV. Although he moved between three prisons during his sentence this kind of discussion only happened on this occasion.

The work of external drug agencies within prison, and of prison treatment groups, was another route by which interviewees could learn about HIV.

> "I went to NA [Narcotics Anonymous] meetings, it is very good and gives you a lot of information about drugs, HIV etc." (28 year old female, held in a central London prison)

> "There were people from a drug agency from outside prison who did HIV education. . . it was good." (36 year old female, imprisoned for seven months)

However, several interviewees indicated that they doubted the intentions behind some of the educational messages, as in the case of the Terrence Higgins Trust leaflets which one prisoner referred to as 'rules'. It is easy to see how intentions may be misconstrued in prison.

> "In XXX prison they show all inmates at reception a video of how to take drugs properly. It wasn't for the prisoners' sake but because they don't want ODs [overdoses] in the prison which would be bad publicity." (35 year old male, imprisoned for one month)

One respondent who was found in possession of a needle and syringe reported that, after being disciplined, the opportunity was used by a prison officer to give him some basic information about HIV.

HIV TESTING

Testing for HIV was not offered routinely to those interviewed. For the majority (25), HIV status or previous experience of HIV testing was not mentioned at all during their imprisonment. This seems to reflect variation in practice between institutions.

> "I was asked whether I knew about AIDS and if I'd been tested at prison A, but not B. I was not asked to have a test at any of the prisons." (32 year old male, imprisoned for nine months)

> "Nobody mentioned anything at X prison, then I went to Y prison, they asked me about my status and if I wanted a test, and then Z prison, not a whisper." (25 year old male, imprisoned for six months)

All of those who were questioned about or offered HIV testing encountered this during the early stages of imprisonment. The question of HIV testing was generally raised by the prison doctor who would ask interviewees whether they were HIV positive or if they had been tested for HIV.

James, a 29 year old Irish man held in a central London prison, was questioned about his HIV status on reception into prison once he had offered information about his drug use.

> "There was this. . . questionnaire right, they asked me where I was born, my religion, any mental disorders, 'anything else' they said, I said 'I'm a drug user', they said 'Do you have Hepatitis?', I said 'B', they then said 'Do you have HIV?' "

Alastair, a 33 year old Scottish man held in a prison in northwest England, was questioned about HIV testing by the doctor on reception, but decided not to disclose how many times he had been tested. He thought once the prison doctor found out he would ask him more questions about his past.

> "They asked me if I was HIV. . . I said 'listen I'm not HIV'. . . they said 'have you been tested?' I said 'yes', 'How many?' I said 'one' even though I've had 13, but I didn't want them raking around my past."

Five interviewees reported that they asked for an HIV test when the issue was raised by the prison doctor. However, not all those who requested a test were given one. Two interviewees, a man and a woman held in central London prisons, maintain that they were refused the opportunity of an HIV test on the grounds of cost. Christine, a 36 year old held in a central London prison, said she asked to be tested for HIV because everything had been "very chaotic" prior to her imprisonment, but the request was turned down by the medical officer "because it's too expensive". Other interviewees reported being discouraged from having an HIV test while they were in prison. One interviewee recounted a conversation with a prison officer about HIV. He told the officer that he had been tested in the past and that he thought he should undergo 'the test' again. The officer told him he would be "better off" waiting until he was released from prison.

Testing Procedure

Of the 44 drug injectors interviewed, 11 were tested for HIV during their last period of imprisonment. Many agreed to be tested because they saw their time in prison as a good opportunity to get a clean bill of health. Others saw the test as aiding their psychological well-being.

> "I wanted the test for some peace of mind." (25 year old male, held in a prison in central London)

One interviewee reported that, after being counselled by a doctor about HIV and the testing procedure, he decided against having an HIV test.

Two people said that they were tested for HIV without their knowledge and consent. Jane, a 29 year old women held in a central London prison, told the doctor on reception into prison that she had Hepatitis C.

> ". . . so they checked me over. . . and the next day they took a blood test."

It was a few weeks before the results of the blood test came back, during which time she was held on the hospital wing.

> "When the test came back they told me it was negative for Hepatitis A and B, and HIV."

Jane had not known that her blood was going to be tested for HIV and had not received counselling about the test.

George, an Italian held in a central London prison, had a girlfriend who died of AIDS several years earlier and was very worried about having an HIV test. On reception into prison he was asked by the prison doctor if he was HIV positive. George told him that he did not know. The doctor told George that "they must find out". George said that he did not want to have the test but "they said I had to". George did not agree to have the test but he believed if he protested further it would be to his disadvantage. "When you are in prison and you start to complain about some things. . . things can become very difficult."

Two interviewees suggested that their consent to being tested was given when they were in a situation where it was difficult for them to make a proper decision about whether or not to be tested. Both were undergoing withdrawal from drugs at the time.

> "I was asked if I wanted the test. I was really withdrawing, I just wanted some drugs so I said yes." (28 year old female, held in a central London prison)

Many of those who were tested (six) were kept on the hospital wing of the prison until the result of their test was known by the prison medical staff. The allocation to the hospital wing to await the result of the test was seen as a kind of additional punishment, in that it meant reduced access to facilities, and that they could not join in normal prison life.

A 35 year old male held in a prison in the Midlands protested at being held on the hospital wing as he was physically fit. He was told that people were always kept "on the isolation" awaiting the results of the test.

Counselling

Interviewees were asked to describe the procedure surrounding their prison HIV test, their interaction with doctors and nurses, and the information, advice and support offered to them.

Of those tested for HIV during their last period of imprisonment, two interviewees did not know whether they had participated in counselling. The majority (6) however were aware that they had not received counselling about HIV when they were tested.

> "The prison doctor asked whether I wanted an HIV test, and I agreed. He said I could have another one in three months time. There was no counselling offered with either test." (39 year old male, imprisoned for 12 months)

> "They [prison medical staff] never told me anything, they just took the blood, they didn't even give me the result. . ." (25 year old male, held in a central London prison)

The above interviewee was held on the hospital wing for two weeks and then relocated to a general wing. His fellow prisoners told him he must be 'clean' (HIV negative) since he had been allowed into a normal location.

Of those who did receive counselling, some mentioned that the quality of counselling was poor.

> "The prison officers who were supposed to counsel the prisoners before HIV tests didn't know enough to counsel drug injectors. They only knew about the homosexual nature of HIV transmission." (29 year old male, held in a prison in northwest England)

Only three of those who were tested for HIV in prison said they had received counselling, one of whom said the doctor who undertook his counselling was not a prison doctor.

> "I was counselled by a doctor for about 15 minutes before having the test. The doctor was from outside of the prison. He also gave me leaflets on HIV." (25 year old male, held in a central London prison)

> "The doctor told me about the effects of having an HIV test, the effects on my life if I was diagnosed HIV positive." (22 year old male, imprisoned for six months)

A 19 year old female prisoner, after agreeing to be tested, had an interview with a psychologist about the possible outcome of the test. She was then informed of the test result by the prison doctor. She commented that she found the whole process to be "very confidential".

Three of the tested group were not informed of the result of the test they had undertaken, and only two respondents received any form of counselling on receipt of the test result.

One respondent who was remanded in custody in a Midlands prison for only three weeks requested to be tested for HIV on the day he was incarcerated. The test was not carried out until the second week of his imprisonment. When the doctor informed him that the result of the test would not be known for two weeks, the prisoner told the doctor that he expected to have been released by then. The doctor then made arrangements for the respondent, once released, to return to the hospital wing and receive the results of the test.

Many of those tested for HIV in prison had prior experience of HIV testing. A diverse range of experiences were described by interviewees concerning the HIV testing procedure in prison. Only one interviewee, however, believed the process had been completed satisfactorily.

EXPERIENCES OF HIV POSITIVE PRISONERS

Of the sample of drug injectors interviewed, two were HIV positive: Steve – a 28 year old Irish man and Alan – a 36 year old from southeast England. Both disclosed their HIV status to the prison doctor on entry into prison.

Alan

Alan, who had been in receipt of a long term methadone maintenance prescription prior to his arrest, was held in police cells for four days before he was allocated to a central London prison. On reception into prison Alan informed the medical officer that he was HIV positive with a history of drug use. The medical officer said that he already knew of these details since they were in the file that accompanied him. By this time Alan was suffering from severe withdrawal effects, but the medical officer said that he could not offer any treatment, adding that Alan should have already suffered the worst effects of withdrawal by this point.

Alan was held on the hospital wing of the prison throughout his three month sentence. He was in a cell by himself and was only allowed out of his cell for thirty minutes a day for exercise.

He was examined on arrival at the hospital wing but received no more medical attention while in prison. During this time he continued to experience physical effects of withdrawal and was unable to sleep.

Once Alan had made contact with his parents he asked them to contact his doctor at the drug dependency unit he had attended for the previous two years. The doctor from this unit contacted the prison authorities to request to see Alan but his request was rejected.

Alan felt the staff in prison were often hostile, especially when he made a request, but generally they just ignored him. He believed the staff displayed little or no understanding of HIV.

Steve

Steve, who was imprisoned for nine months had contrasting experiences being HIV positive and imprisoned. His initial experiences were in a central London prison while remanded.

> "They treated me at first as if they didn't believe me. At first when I went into prison I was very sick – they didn't give me methadone. The way they looked at it was that when I told them I was HIV they said 'well everybody tells us that, they just say it to get drugs.'"

Steve was put on a normal location in the prison and given Valium for three days. He continued to protest to the prison doctor that he was HIV positive but throughout the doctor refused to examine him. However, after six weeks, he convinced the doctor to take his blood to have it tested for HIV. During this period, Steve's health deteriorated.

When the results of his test were known, Steve was seen by a specialist from outside of the prison.

> "He [outside specialist] came in every week for HIV prisoners, he was a very understanding man, he took blood from me. . . and he told me that my T-cell count was very low. . . he asked me if I had ever had AZT [Zidovudine]."

After four months on remand, Steve was sentenced and allocated to a prison in East Anglia. On reception, the doctor was given a letter marked for his attention which detailed Steve's medical record.

> "The doctor examined me, then I was put on normal location. He gave me things to relax me because I was still very stressed, but anything I needed health wise he gave me. I got vitamins and all that, you know, fruit and milk."

Steve found his new prison to be a very different environment. He believed the officers were very supportive and always willing to talk.

> "There were four different counsellors, [prison] officers learning to be HIV counsellors. The medical officers used to come and ask me if it was alright for these officers to come and talk to me. . . They wanted to know more about HIV and I was pleased to do it, you know."

The experiences appear to vary according to the institution in which interviewees were held, a difference commented on by Steve.

> *"The prison in London was too busy, too overstretched, too overworked, everything. The food is bad and they don't care. When you go to a prison outside of London it's a world of difference, they look at you as a whole and are very understanding."*

Summary

There was considerable variation in the provision of education and information about HIV and AIDS, and these did not appear to be routinely offered. Only nine interviewees reported seeing a video, and only four were given a leaflet about HIV and AIDS. Those who did see the video described a number of problems with different aspects of the video presentation. On the other hand, many were able to find out about AIDS through their contacts with prison officers and community based agencies.

Many respondents were questioned about their HIV status and previous experiences of HIV testing on reception into prison. Eleven were tested for HIV during their last period of imprisonment. The majority agreed or requested to be tested and prison was viewed as a good opportunity to get a 'clean bill of health'. There seems to be a lack of consistent attention to counselling.

Of those tested, the majority said that they had not been counselled. This cannot be accounted for by prisoners' ignorance of counselling, for many of them had been counselled when they were tested outside of prison and understood what it was. Those who were tested for HIV were often held in the prison hospital wing until the result of the test was known. There are problems with the provision of information about test results. Three of those tested for HIV were not informed of the result of the test and the majority did not receive counselling on receipt of the test result.

We have previously reported that some prisoners appear to be tested without their knowledge or consent (Turnbull et al 1993), or are tested when their physical condition is such that they cannot come to a proper decision. This still appears to happen to some prisoners who are tested for HIV without their knowledge when blood is taken for other tests, or who are in a state of withdrawal when asked to give their consent for an HIV test.

Two respondents were known to be HIV positive by the prison authorities. Their experiences of imprisonment as known HIV positive prisoners were contrasting, which appeared to be related to the institution in which they were held.

CHAPTER 7

OVERVIEW AND CONCLUSIONS

There is continued concern surrounding drug use and related HIV risk behaviour in custodial institutions. While some commentators point to the moderate advances that have been made in the care and treatment of HIV positive inmates and in the detoxification of those who are dependent on drugs, others suggest that these measures are to date, patchy in coverage and are often inadequate (Advisory Council on the Misuse of Drugs 1993; Gore et al 1993; Ross et al 1994).

Our previous research has shown that prisons are problematic places for drug users and injectors. Many of the conclusions and recommendations made before by ourselves are still pertinent. These include:

- Consideration should be given to the provision of cleaning agents to disinfect needles and syringes, with ease of access, confidentiality and instructions on use.

- Treatment options for drug users in prison should be of equal range and quality as those in the community. For those drug injectors who pass through the prison system, there needs to be much better continuity of care between prison and the community.

- A clear concerted policy and programme is required at all levels in the Prison Service. Within each custodial institution there needs to be a comprehensive package of education, prevention, help, care and treatment for HIV and AIDS, drug use and related problems.

(Turnbull et al 1991)

The World Health Organization (WHO) Global Programme on AIDS issued guidelines in 1993 on "HIV Infection and AIDS in Prisons", which highlight the particular problems of drug use and injecting. A number of recommendations were made concerning treatment for those with problematic drug use and the prevention of HIV transmission by injecting drug use. Specific recommendations were made about methadone and the distribution of effective viricidal agents. The WHO guidelines recommended that prisoners on methadone maintenance prior to imprisonment should be able to continue this treatment when in prison, and where methadone maintenance is available to opiate-dependent individuals in the community, this treatment should also be available in prisons. The distribution of bleach or other viricidal agents with specific detailed instructions on their use was also recommended. It was also suggested that in countries where clean syringes and needles are made available to injecting drug users in the community, consideration should be given to providing clean injecting equipment during detention and on release to prisoners who request this (The World Health Organization 1993).

Study findings

> *The findings of this study suggest that drug use in prisons is widespread. Drug problems in prison may now be developing more rapidly than the current ability of prison authorities to respond effectively. The urgency of the need to introduce effective measures is highlighted by the recent outbreak of HIV and Hepatitis B infection in a Scottish prison (Scottish Affairs Committee 1994).*

We have tried to examine drug use in prison from the perspective of the prisoner. Other reports have looked at the action that is planned within the prison service, or at the characteristics of drug users in the prison system. We feel that an understanding of the current nature and effectiveness of the prison response to drug use and to HIV infection, is incomplete without an assessment from the point of view of those who are the targets of interventions and the recipients of services.

The people who were interviewed were long term drug users, having much experience of drug use, prisons, and treatment provision both inside and outside of prison.

All respondents continued using drugs while in prison. Prisons constitute unique surroundings for drug use. Although the scale of individual drug use and injecting may decline in comparison with the community, prison drug use brings its own dangers, including the use of adulterated drugs, unsterile syringes, and debt – with the possibility of violence and bullying for both prisoners, and given the nature of prison drug markets, often for their spouses and friends in the community.

Individual supplies of drugs are shared with cell mates and other prisoners in a reciprocal relationship which helps maintain supply – showing the interdependence of drug users in prison.

Drug use in prison cannot be seen as an isolated phenomenon; drugs are an entrenched part of prison society and economy, and affect many aspects of prison life – including reception and discharge, association, exercise, work, visits, health, security, and personal safety. Drug use affects prisoners and prison staff, and their relationships with one another. As well as prisons posing problems for drug users, drug use poses major problems for the prison service.

> *It is important that all custodial institutions develop and implement adequate policies and practices concerning drugs and drug users. Given the wide ramifications of drug use, all policies and practices in prisons might now have to be considered in the light of their influence on drug use. In particular it may be necessary to consider how policy and practice may contribute to a reduction in drug use and to lessening the harmful consequences for drug using prisoners, other prisoners and prison staff.*

> *It is important that prisons attempt to interrupt the continuation of problematic drug use by making it less attractive, and where it continues, to reduce its harmful consequences. The provision of a wide range of treatment opportunities will go some way to providing an alternative to continued drug use.*

Drug users continue to use drugs when imprisoned for a number of reasons. For some it is a fundamental and 'natural' behaviour, while for others it is necessary and unavoidable to alleviate withdrawal symptoms or longer term insomnia. Strong impressions were gained from the interviews of the lack of adequate and consistent provision of treatment and other services for people with drug problems who are imprisoned.

> *Drug users, on the whole, believed that the medication and treatment available was inadequate, and said that they experienced severe withdrawal symptoms as a result. Continued drug use among prisoners has to be understood in the context of the lack of adequate services for helping and treating this group.*

Many opportunities for intervention occur, but are presently being missed. Unless a wide range of services are offered there is little incentive for drug users to disclose drug use, cooperate with prison authorities, and stop using drugs. Indeed, there were examples of people who intended to use their imprisonment to stop using drugs, but who found that with both a lack of support and the extensive use of drugs by other prisoners, they were unable to do so.

> *Measures must be undertaken to encourage the disclosure of problematic drug use at intake into prison. An incentive for individuals to disclose drug use would be the provision of adequate treatment opportunities.*

From the point of view of the imprisoned drug user, it may not be in their interest to disclose problematic drug use at intake, until he or she is aware of the kinds of help available within a particular institution. Furthermore, individual drug use may occur in an intermittent (and sometimes ongoing) manner throughout a period of imprisonment. Therefore, whilst the intake period is probably an opportunity for disclosure and discussion of treatment options, opportunities should also be available at other times.

> *Measures must be taken to encourage the disclosure of problematic drug use throughout the period of imprisonment.*

There is a clear difficulty for prison staff in balancing the need to maintain discipline, and the need to make treatment and help available. However, provision of treatment and help in prison is unlikely to be successful if it is within the climate of disciplinary action regarding possession. It is doubtful whether treatment given under compulsion or other threat leads to long term successful outcomes. Proposals to introduce mandatory urine screening to detect drug use, if accompanied by disciplinary action, would not be conducive to creating a proper climate for provision of treatment and help. The use of such measures would also be counterproductive when used as a measure to control drug free wings and expel those who have not been able to comply with the treatment regime.

> *Given the major health and personal problems that may be associated with drug use, the discovery of drug use and injecting by the prison authorities should be used primarily as an opportunity for referral to treatment and the provision of harm reduction information and education rather than as an opportunity for disciplinary action.*

There is considerable variety of practice between and within prisons. From the client's perspective there was little indication of the implementation of clear and consistent practice. The way forward in prisons must be to pursue a programme of implementation of effective policies and practices. The process of setting targets and outcomes in the NHS should be similarly required of those providing health care in the custodial setting.

> *Planning mechanisms involving minimum standards of service provision, target setting, quality controls, and monitoring may be useful in implementing prison drugs and HIV policy. There is an immediate need for the setting of national standards with targets for their implementation. Each institution should agree minimum standards of services and targets within an overall contract to provide health care services.*

Health care provision for drug users in prison is not equivalent to that available in the community.

> *Professional medical and nursing associations may wish to consider whether it is unethical to withhold in prison, a standard of care that is available in the community.*

Current substitute prescribing within prison is mainly the provision of symptomatic treatment (using tranquillisers) or short term methadone detoxification (seven days or less). The lack of availability of longer term or maintenance prescribing is unrealistic both in terms of the withdrawal symptoms that may occur over a longer period, in terms of the cycle of re-addiction that may occur with the intermittent use of opiates during imprisonment, and with the risks associated with injecting drugs. There is now considerable evidence that in community settings methadone maintenance is effective in reducing levels of opiate consumption and in reducing HIV risk behaviour (Ward et al 1992).

> *Attention should be given to the development of suitable longer term methadone treatment within prisons.*

The lack of availability of longer term methadone treatment is incompatible with the treatment that many of the people in this study had received immediately prior to imprisonment.

> *Denial of continuity of treatment from the community into prison is unsatisfactory for the individual prisoner and undermines the programme of treatment pursued in the community.*

Some of the barriers to the effective development and delivery of drug services stem from conflicts between different categories of prison staff. Problematic drug use seemed to be viewed by some staff as a moral issue.

> *Prison staff need to be informed of the aims and objectives of the provision of drug treatment in prison.*

A third of injectors who took part in the study continued to inject, although their frequency of injecting was lower than that prior to imprisonment.

> *The risks of infection from injecting were extremely high. In looking in more detail at how, when, and where injecting took place it is apparent that risks associated with injecting in prison are considerably greater than outside. Many of those who injected in prison shared injecting equipment.*

Drug injectors who were imprisoned had a limited conception of the term 'sharing'. 'Sharing' had a very precise meaning, and referred to instances when other people were present and the needles and syringes were passed between people. It does not coincide with what a virologist or epidemiologist might define as sharing, in that it did not include using syringes that might have been used on a previous occasion (this was simply "using old works"), nor did it refer to sharing of injecting solutions (as in back or front loading, or the shared use of containers) or filters or other paraphernalia. This has important implications for educational initiatives in that they will need to address drug users' conceptions of syringe sharing behaviour.

> *In addition to the immediate sharing of syringes, drug injecting prisoners need to be reminded that risks arise from the re-use of any syringes that have already been used by others, and of other risks, such as the sharing of filters, spoons, water, and injecting solutions.*

The paucity of harm reduction materials and the continuation of high risk practices indicate the urgent need for the development of harm reduction measures. Decontaminants are an acceptable option for cleaning injecting equipment. When used correctly, they may help prevent HIV transmission.

> *Drug injectors' attempts to clean injecting equipment that had already been used were pitiful and inadequate. The provision of decontaminants is essential and should be implemented with appropriate evaluation. Harm reduction materials must be available at the time of use, and in this respect it is important to note that much of the injecting occurred in cells.*

Some prisons have reportedly begun to make available to prisoners, bleach in liquid or tablet form and other decontaminants (Milton). Recent reports of the lack of in situ effectiveness of bleach as a protection against HIV infection suggest that bleach may not always in practice be used in the correct manner (i.e. full strength and with soaking for the appropriate length of time). Doubts must be raised about the potential improper use of some decontaminants (e.g. bleach tablets) which are not provided at proper strength.

It is unclear whether these decontaminants are effective against other blood borne diseases such as Hepatitis. Indeed, it is important to know the extent of Hepatitis B and C infection within the prison population.

> *There is an urgent need for the Directorate of Health Care Services for Prisoners, with the advice of the Public Health Laboratory Service, to advise prisoners about safe decontaminants to prevent infection with Hepatitis B, C, and HIV.*

There is considerable variation between institutions in their practices regarding drug injectors and HIV infection, and even variation within prisons. Eleven respondents were tested for HIV during their last period of imprisonment, the majority viewing prison as a good opportunity to get a 'clean bill of health'. However, there seems to be a lack of consistent attention to counselling. Experiences of imprisonment for those known to be HIV positive were contrasting, which appeared to be related to the institution in which they were held.

This might be connected with the variable implementation of Prison Health Service policy. This may show that the evidence of our earlier study – which found problems with the provision of education and information, HIV testing, consent and counselling – is still pertinent. On the positive side, there is evidence that it is possible for drug injectors and for people who are potentially HIV positive, to be managed within prison in an understanding manner. But ultimately, the rather diverse state of affairs seems to indicate many difficulties in pursuing a coherent policy throughout the prison system. Issues of HIV and AIDS are too important to be left to institutional or individual idiosyncrasy.

There need to be proper standards for HIV testing procedures and quality control, and the means for their implementation against agreed targets, within an overall contracting framework. As in our earlier report, consideration should be given to HIV testing being provided by external bodies experienced in counselling and testing.

There was also considerable variation in the provision of education and information about HIV/AIDS, and this did not appear to be routinely offered. From the point of view of the recipient, HIV education within prisons appears to lack credibility. Those providing the education, the information given, and the methods used, placed within the context of the prison environment, make it difficult to conduct meaningful education initiatives from the point of view of the prisoners.

It may be desirable for there to be more extensive involvement of outside agencies in the provision of drugs/HIV education within prisons. A review of current HIV education in prisons is needed which should take into account when, where, and how education is provided.

In many countries attention is now being given to the role that drug users and drug injectors may play in influencing their peers. The evidence from this study is that the use of drugs is embedded in a matrix of functional, social and situational influences that contribute to a particular social etiquette of prison drug use. Drug acquisition and use are rarely solitary activities, and drug users in prison depend on each other to obtain and use drugs. This indicates the potential for peer education. At its simplest, peer education requires educators and counsellors to persuade drug users to pass on prevention messages to others. In more sophisticated versions, it may involve special training for drug users to provide them with knowledge and communication skills.

Educational initiatives might focus on the opportunities to use existing drug users and their social networks within prison as possible points for the dissemination of information and advice. These networks may be an appropriate vehicle for peer education programmes delivered by credible sources.

References

Advisory Council on the Misuse of Drugs (1988). AIDS and Drug Misuse Part 1. London: HMSO.

Advisory Council on the Misuse of Drugs (1993). AIDS and Drug Misuse Update. London: HMSO.

Bird AG, Gore SM, Jolliffe DW, Burns SM. (1992) Anonymous HIV surveillance in Saughton Prison, Edinburgh. AIDS, 6, 623–628.

Brewer TF, Derrickson J. (1992) AIDS in Prison: A review of epidemiology and preventive policy. AIDS, 6: 623–628.

Covell RG, Frischer M, Taylor A, Goldberg SG, McKeganey N, Bloor M. (1993) Prison experience of injecting drug users in Glasgow. Drug and Alcohol Dependence, 32, 9–14.

Dolan KA, Donoghoe MC, Stimson GV. (1990) Drug injecting and syringe sharing in custody and the community: an exploratory survey of HIV risk behaviour. The Howard Journal of Criminal Justice, 29 (3), 177–186.

Donoghoe MC, Stimson GV, Dolan KA. (1992) Syringe Exchange in England, An Overview. The Tufnell Press, London.

Farrell M, Strang J. (1991) Drugs, HIV and prisons. British Medical Journal, 302, 1477–1478.

Gore SM, Bird AG. (1993) No escape: HIV transmission in jail. British Medical Journal, 307, 147–148.

Grund JPC. (1993) Drug use as a social ritual. Rotterdam: Instituut Voor Verslavingsonderzoek.

Harding T, Schaller G. (1992) HIV/AIDS and Prisons: Updating and Policy Review. Report for the World Health Organization Global Programme on AIDS, Geneva.

Her Majesty's Chief Inspector of Prisons. (1992) Report April 1991 – March 1992. London: HMSO.

Her Majesty's Prison Service. (1991) Caring for Drug Users. London: Home Office.

Home Office Statistical Bulletin. (1993) Statistics of drug addicts, UK, notified to the Home Office 1992. London: HMSO.

Jose B, Friedman SR, Neaigus A, Curtis R, Grund JPC, Goldstein, Ward TP, Des Jarlias DC. (1993) Syringe-mediated drug sharing (backloading): a new risk factor for HIV among injecting drug users. AIDS, 7: 1653–1660.

Keene J, Stimson GV, Jones S, Parry-Langdon N. Evaluation of syringe-exchange for HIV prevention among injecting drug users in rural and urban areas of Wales. Addiction 1993; 88: 1063–70.

Maden A, Swinton M, Gunn J. (1990a) Drug dependence in prison. British Medical Journal, 302, 880.

Maden A, Swinton M, Gunn J. (1990b) Women in prison and use of illicit drugs before. British Medical Journal, 301, 1133.

Pickering H, Stimson GV. (1993) Syringe sharing in prison. The Lancet, 342, 621–622.

Power KG, Marakova I, Rowlands A, Mckee KL, Anslow PJ, Kilfedder C. (1992) Intravenous drug use and HIV transmission amongst inmates in Scottish prisons. British Journal of Addiction 87, 35–45.

Power R. (1989) Participant observation and its place in the study of illicit drug abuse. British Journal of Addiction, 84, 43–52.

Ross M, Grossman AB, Murdoch S, Bundey R, Golding J, Purchase S, et al. Prison: shield from threat, or threat to survival? BMJ 1994; 308: 1092–5.

Scottish Affairs Committee. (1994) Drug Abuse in Scotland, First Report. Volume 1. London: HMSO.

Stimson GV, Alldritt LJ, Dolan KA, Donoghoe MC, Lart RA. (1988) Injecting Equipment Exchange Schemes: Final Report. Monitoring Research Group, Goldsmiths' College, London.

Turnbull PJ, Dolan KA, Stimson GV. (1991) Prisons, HIV and AIDS: Risks and experiences in custodial care. Horsham: AVERT.

Turnbull PJ, Stimson GV, Dolan KA. (1992) Prevalence of HIV infection among ex-prisoners in England. British Medical Journal, 304, 90–91.

Turnbull PJ, Stimson GV. (1993) Prisons: Heterosexuals in a risk environment. In: Sherr L (eds) AIDS and the Heterosexual Population. Reading: Harwood Academic Publishers.

Ward J, Mattick R, Hall W. (1992) Key Issues in Methadone Maintenance Treatment. Sydney: New South Wales University Press.

World Health Organization, Global Programme on AIDS. (1993) WHO Guidelines on HIV Infection and AIDS in Prisons. Geneva: WHO.